Special thanks to
Robin Dictenberg
Dave Dye
John LaMacchia
Bob Miller
Hugues Pinguet
Anne-Rose Schlutbohm
Anne Telford
Yuji Tokuda
and
Keiichi Uemura
for their professional advice and assistance.

Contents

Contents

Contents

Contents

Lürzer's Archive Special
200 Best Ad Photographers worldwide 10/11
(ISBN 978-3-902393-10-4)

Publisher & Editor: Walter Lürzer **Editor-in-chief:** Michael Weinzettl **Production Manager:** Christian Hrdlicka **Editorial Assistants:** Andrea Brandner, Victoria Morgan, Stephanie Sutanto **Layout & Pre-Press:** Ulli Singer **Marketing & Salesmanager:** Sandra Lehnst **Sales Representatives:** Kate Brown, Claudia Coffman, Sheila King, Diana Dragomir, Carina Wicke

Administration/Editorial Office: Lürzer GmbH, Keinergasse 29, 1030 Vienna, Austria, phone: (43) 1 715 24 24, office@luerzersarchive.com, submission@luerzersarchive.com
Printers: Niederösterreichisches Pressehaus, Druck- und Verlagsgesellschaft mbH, Gutenbergstraße 12, 3100 St. Pölten, Austria, phone: (43) 2742 802-0 www.np-druck.at

Distributors:
Argentina: La Paragrafica, tool@paragrafica.com.ar **Australia:** Selectair Distribution Services, sales@selectair.com.au **Brazil:** Livraria Freebook Ltda., manuel@freebook.com.br; Casa Ono Com. e Imp. Ltda., casaono@uol.com.br; Open Books, romeu@openbooks.com.br **Bulgaria:** Milen Marchev, archive@milenmarchev.com **Canada:** Keng Seng Enterprises Inc., canada@kengseng.com **China:** Beijing Designersbooks, import01@designerbooks.com.cn **Colombia:** Diseño Y Tecnica, distecnica@hotmail.com; Foto Colombia, stamayo@fotocolombia.com **Costa Rica:** BAUM S.A., baumsa@racsa.

co.cr **Czech Republik:** ADC Czech Republic, info@adc-czech.cz **Denmark:** Tegnecenter, info@tegnecenter.dk **Dominican Republic:** Portfolio Group, wendolyn@portfoliodr.com **Finland:** Suomalainen Kirjakauppa, tom.nordstrom@suomalainenkk.fi **France:** Lürzer's Archive, (Interlocuteur Français), office@luerzersarchive.com **Germany:** IPS Datenservice GmbH, abo-archiv@ips-d.de **Ghana:** Chini Productions Ltd., archive@chiniproductions.com **Greece:** Studio Bookshop, office@studiobookshop.com **Hong Kong:** Keng Seng Trading & Co. Ltd., lawrence@kengseng.com **Hungary:** Librotrade Kft., periodicals@librotrade.hu **India:** ISBD, sbds@bol.net.in **Indonesia:** Basheer Graphic Books, abdul @basheergraphic.com **Italy:** Ellesette, ellesette@ellesette.com; RED, info @redonline.it **Japan:** DIP, erol@dip-inc.com **Korea:** Yi Sam Sa, yss23k@kornet.net **Latvia:** Valters un Rapa, santa@valtersunrapa.lv **Malaysia:** The Other Bookstore, hajaotherbookstore@yahoo.com **Moldavia:** Mesageria D&D, mesageriadd@gmail.com **Mexico:** Rolando de la Piedra, hosrpb@prodigy.net.mx **Netherlands/Belgium:** Bruil & Van de Staaij, info@bruil.info **New Zealand:** The Magazine Marketing Company Ltd, stuart.shepherd@tmmc.co.nz **Nigeria:** Chini Productions, archive@chiniproductions.com **Norway:** Luth & Co/Font Shop, info@luth.no **Panama:** Latin Magazine Group, csmith@publicist.com **Peru:** Libreria Mediatica, mediatica@ec-red.com **Poland:** VFP Communications, kehrt@media.com.pl **Portugal:** Marka Lda., apoio.clientes@marka.pt; Tema Lda., belmiro@mail.telepac.pt **Romania:** Prior Books, ion.arzoiu@prior.ro **Russia:** IndexMarket, info@indexmarket.ru **Singapore:** Basheer Graphic Books, abdul@basheergraphic.com; Page One, pageone@singnet.com.sg **Slovakia:** Archive F.K., predplatne@predplatne.net **Slovenia / Albania / Bosnia & Herzegovina / Croatia / Macedonia / Serbia & Montenegro:** New Moments D.O.O., ideas@newmoment.si **South Africa:** Biblioteq, rotem_is@mac.com; International Subscription Services, isscc@icon.co.za **Spain:** Comercial Atheneum S.A., suscri.bcn@atheneum.com; Promotora De Prensa, evelazquez@promopress.es **Sri Lanka:** Leo Burnett Solutions Inc., swarna_goonetillke@leoburnett.lk **Sweden:** Svenska Interpress, info@interpress.se **Taiwan:** Far Go Chen Co. Ltd., fargo899@ms35.hinet.net **Thailand:** B2S Co. Ltd., YiSorrapong@b2s.co.th **Turkey:** Alternatif, alternatif@grafikkitaplari.com; Evrensel, evrensely@superonline.com **Ukraine:** DAN, olga@ceo.com.ua; All-Ukrainan Advertising Coalition, mial@adcoalition.org.ua **United Arab Emirates / Bahrein / Kuwait / Oman / Saudi Arabia / Qatar:** MBR Bookshop LLC, asoniemirates.net.ae **United Kingdom / Ireland:** Central Books, sasha@centralbooks.com; Timscris, kb@luerzersarchive.com **Uruguay:** Graffiti S.R.L., graffiti@faslink.com.uy **United States:** Lürzer's Archive Inc., custsvc_archive @fulcoinc.com **Venezuela:** April Itriago, april.itriago@gmail.com **All other countries:** IPS, Meckenheim, Germany, (English speaking), sub-archive@ips-d.de

How to use your Archive:
Guide to symbols: ◻: Photographer ⌂: Advertising Agency ⎯▷: Art Director ✎: Digital Artist ♡: Client

All editorial material reproduced in Lürzer's Archive Special are categorized by product, e.g. "Animals." Product groups are shown alphabetically. Every editorial page is cross-referenced with an Archive number, the first two digits indicating the year in which the special was published, and the second three digits being continuous page numbers for that particular product group. For example, 200bph 10.001 under "Animals" indicates the Volume published in 2010, and page 1 of that product group.

Submission is now open for our next specials, "200 Best Product Designers 2010/11" and "200 Best Web Designers 2010/11." For further information, please visit www.luerzersarchive.com/submission

Cover page:
◻: Julien Vonier ⌂: Advico Young & Rubicam, Zurich ♡: Zoo Zurich

The facts behind the figures.

These past two years have, not surprisingly, been tough ones for commercial photographers. In an article entitled "The Cloud is Falling," published on the website SportsShooter.com, an online resource for sports photography, Pulitzer prize-winning ad and editorial photographer Vincent Laforet tried to come up with a bit of consolation as well as advice for his colleagues: "The recession is already having an noticeable effect ...," he wrote in this review of declining advertising expenditures and their impact on ad photography. "Large, lucrative campaigns are being put aside, rates are going down as are production budgets, and everyone is already feeling it in that market. I spoke with an agent at a well respected agency representing many of the top advertising photographers in the business and was told that jobs are down 20–30% so far this year, and that a few of their photographers have not gotten a single job in more than 6 months ... that fewer original ads were being shot – winning a bid was more than often highly influenced by being the lowest bidder, and that advertisers were extending rights from previous shoots ... Furthermore the agent told me that they saw this trend continuing for the next two years or so. Scary. So please, go shoot weddings, they're great."

This article was posted on June 30, 2008. After that, of course, things went from bad to worse.

So how has this dismal development affected the biannual volume you are now holding in your hands? Some of the facts and figures detailed below speak for themselves, while others may be more ambiguous and, possibly, not a direct result of the difficult economic climate. First of all, the number of submissions was up – from 5,709 in the previous 200 Best Ad Photographers to 6,539 in the volume at hand. As always, these submissions came from photographers who had been either nominated by art directors of well-known ad agencies from around the world, or were among those featured in Lürzer's Archive magazine or in an earlier volume of our 200 Best series (thus earning them a Top 50 position in our Photographers Ranking at www.luerzersarchive.com). From these, our international jury selected a total of 572 images – as opposed to 813 in the previous issue – shot by the 200 photographers that take the honors in this volume. This jury, to which we should like to express our sincere gratitude for the invaluable work they put into this selection, was made up as follows:

- Robin Dictenberg of Greenhouse Reps, New York
- Dave Dye, Commissioning Editor, Dye Holloway Murray, London
- John LaMacchia, Associate Creative Director, Ogilvy, New York
- Bob Miller, photographer and co-founder of Lensmodern, London
- Hugues Pinguet, Art Director, BETC Euro RSCG, Paris
- Anne-Rose Schlutbohm, former editor of Profession Photographe, Paris
- Anne Telford, Editor-at-large, Communication Arts, Palo Alto
- Yuji Tokuda, Art Director, Canaria, Tokyo
- Keiichi Uemura, Creative Director, Saatchi & Saatchi Fallon, Tokyo
- Michael Weinzettl, Editor-in-chief, Lürzer's Archive, Berlin

As in all three 200 Best volumes published to date, the USA boasts the largest number of photographers, accounting for 51 of the 200. That's 15 fewer than the 66 US photographers represented in the book that came out two years ago. The UK is still in 2nd place, now with a crop of 32, up 6 from Vol. 08/09, while Germany comes in 3rd again, this time with 27 (+12) photographers to its credit. Next is Australia, slipping 5 from its previous count of 14, and only then does the sequence of countries change compared to last time. While 5th place in 08/09 went to Brazil with 9 photographers, this position is now taken by the Netherlands with 8 (unchanged), a slot it shares with Singapore, which has now doubled its tally of photographers. Japan has 7 (up by 2), putting it just ahead of Canada and Italy, both with 6 (also 2 lower than previously). Further down the country ranking come Brazil, India and New Zealand, with 5 photographers each, France and South Africa (with 4 respectively), Argentina, Hong Kong, Russia and Spain (each with 3), Belgium, Romania and Switzerland (2 apiece) and, finally, Emirates, Austria, Denmark, Finland and Poland, each of them with a single photographer among the 200 showcased in this book.

The most striking change is the fact that, of these 200 photographers, a total of 110 did not feature in the previous book, and just 17 of them appeared in 200 Best Ad Photographers worldwide 06/07, the volume before last. Which means, of course, that there are a lot of new discoveries for you to make.

As for the our distribution of the book, a total of 30,000 copies will be circulated to art buyers throughout the world by our distributors in 35 countries. Additionally, 15 copies of each issue will be mailed out on behalf of each photographer featured. Each will also be represented by a Personal Showcase at www.luerzersarchive.com, where photographers can upload 12 selected images of their best work to a website boasting 10 million hits and 100,000 visitors a month.

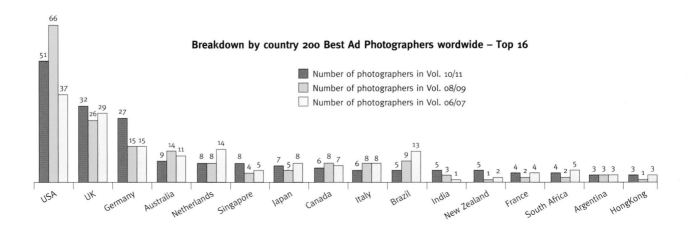

Breakdown by country 200 Best Ad Photographers wordwide – Top 16

- Number of photographers in Vol. 10/11
- Number of photographers in Vol. 08/09
- Number of photographers in Vol. 06/07

The art director is buying not only your talent but also your attitude.

Bob Miller, one of the judges of this selection of outstanding photography from around the world, began his career as a full-time photographer in 1978 and, for the last thirty years, has managed to juggle major photographic advertising and editorial assignments in America and Europe with his own personal photographic projects. Throughout his career, Bob has been the recipient of numerous photographic awards, among them two golds, one silver, and seventeen merits in the Association of Photographers Awards; two silvers for the best black & white campaign two years running in the Campaign Press Awards; three Communications Arts Magazine awards in the USA; a gold award for Audi in the French Design and Art Direction book; and a silver D&AD Award for his photography for Royal Mail Stamps. Bob is familiar with several old black and white printing techniques, and spends many hours in his own darkroom. Over the last couple of years, he has embraced digital imagery, using Photoshop to produce exceptional digital prints. Bob's personal work has been exhibited regularly at a number of photographic galleries in America and Europe. Bob was the founder of lensmodern.com and in the past served on the AOP Council and the Association of Photographers' Awards Committee for two years each. In the following, Bob responds to questions put to him by Michael Weinzettl.

L.A.: Bob, you have been a full-time photographer for 32 years now. How has the business changed over the course of this time?

Bob Miller: Enormous question, enormous changes ... I could write a book on this subject. Before I became a photographer I was an art director at CDP, Byfield Mead and then FGA where I ended up as head of art. In the seventies at CDP there was no competitive estimating. Most of the time, there were no estimates. All the agency wanted was great photographs and great ideas. No one got blamed if the shoot didn't work out. You would just go back and do it again. Clients respected agencies and the creative process. No accountmen or clients were allowed on a shoot and, generally, you could use any photographer in the world. In those days, there were only three main types of media – press, posters, and TV. And there were only four TV channels. Now, there is the internet and hundreds of TV channels. Advertising campaigns are international, and there is very little brand advertising any more. And agencies and clients are scared, especially in the present economic climate. This fear factor doesn't help good photography. It has led to clients and agencies not trusting one another, or not trusting the photographer. Clients will screw the photographer on price but are prepared to pay for ten agency and client personnel to turn up on a shoot. And, nowadays, everyone has an opinion and an attitude. They all think they can write a great ad/commercial or take a great photograph. They lack the patience to allow an idea to grow and to let a photographer exhaust the creative possibilities. Whereas, in the past, British photographers could rely on the UK market for most of their work, now photographers from around the world are all competing for the big jobs at home and abroad. Whenever you're asked to

Bob Miller.

estimate on a job, there are usually five others quoting as well. Of course, things have changed massively on the technical side as well. Fortunately for me, when I started taking photographs in the early 80s, processing e6 transparency film was no longer done by hand. There was very new automatic processing machinery, and it was important to get the right person processing your film. But going digital has changed everything. Suddenly, everyone can take photographs. Self-focus, auto-exposure, changing ASA, no filters – everybody can create and express themselves with a camera now. We also have the merging of film and still photography with the Red camera and the Canon Eos 5D Mk11. Directors and cameramen will become photographers, and photographers will become directors. Obviously, the digital camera would not have been so successful without the development of Photoshop and all the new digital printers. This has brought about another big change. Photographers can now be totally in control of an image from the beginning to the finished print. Sadly, many of the old processes are slowly dying out. Hopefully, in the art market there will still be a place for traditional printing, from dyes and silver bromide prints through to platinum prints.

L.A.: How did you start out as a photographer?

Bob Miller: Like a lot of young children of my generation, I was given a Kodak Brownie when I was about eight and I loved it. At art school, I was taught by a great photographer, Keith Paisley, who had just left the Royal College of Art and had terrific energy. He was the first person to get me really engaged with photography. However, I had a talent for graphic design and chose to go into advertising. My love of photography never left me, though. Being an art director allowed me to work with some wonderful

Image from a Docker brand slacks campaign shot by Bob Miller.

From a California Wine campaign.

photographers, and I learned a lot from just watching them. Lester Bookbinder was the best. His intensity, sensitivity and creativity were unique. In the early eighties, I made the decision to become a photographer while I was head of art at FGA. I bought myself an old MPP 5x4 camera and, with invaluable advice from Rolph Gobits and a lab owner called Paul Gatt, I started shooting. I had a very young family to support and there was a period when I was teaching and art directing as well as taking pictures until, eventually, I was able to become a full-time photographer.

L.A.:. Was it easier to get into photography back then than it is now?

Bob Miller: My entry into photography was made easier because art directors had heard of me, and some were friends who wanted to help me establish myself – although, obviously, I still had to prove myself to them. But, yes, I think it was easier for everybody in those days. There weren't so many trying to get into the business. I think the technical aspect frightened a lot of people off.

L.A.: Who were your photographic heroes when you were starting out?

Bob Miller: On the advertising side the really big guys back then were Irving Penn, Henry Sandbank, Guy Bourdin, Sam Haskins, Art Kane, Donald Silverstein, and Lester Bookbinder. And then there were John Claridge, Barney Edwards, Peter Webb, Adrian Flowers, Rolph Gobits, and David Thorpe. On a more personal note, I loved Andre Kertesz, Paul Strand, Walker Evans, Edward Curtis, Richard Avedon, Horst P. Horst, Bill Brandt, Arnold Newman, Josef Sudek, Edward Steichen, Alfred Stieglitz, and Diane Arbus.

L.A.: Did you ever meet any of them?

Bob Miller: I worked with John Claridge, Barney Edwards, Peter Webb, Adrian Flowers, Lester Bookbinder, Rolph Gobits, David Thorpe, Derek Coutts, and Helmut Newton. You learn so much when you're working with great photographers.

L.A.: What, to you, is a good photograph?

Bob Miller: I look for good composition that is simple and graphic but that has a human, emotional element in it. Mainly, I look for an image that shows me a different point of view and surprises me. There are two quotes that I feel answer your question. The first is by Henri Cartier-Bresson: "Only a fraction of a camera's possibility interests me, the marvelous mixture of emotion and geometry in a single instant." The second quote is by Emile Zola: "It is not the tree, the countenance, the scene offered to me in a picture that touches me. It is the man whom I find in the work, the powerful individual who has known how to create alongside God's world a personal world which my eyes will never forget and which they will recognize everywhere."

L.A.: What does the art director have to bring to the cooperation with a photographer?

Bob Miller: The layout is just the start of the creative process. The art director has to be open to ideas. He must want to use you. He must be cool, and not panic if things are going wrong. He has to trust you and allow you to express yourself but must always remember what the image is communicating and what he is trying to say with the ad. Once he and the photographer have committed to an image, he has to support the decision when he is dealing with his agency and the client.

L.A.: How would you define the roles of art director/photographer in an ideal collaboration?

Bob Miller: You both have to respect one another and trust one another. The art director generally wants what the photographer has to offer. He is not only buying your talent but the attitude you have to your work. He should explain what he is after, and then let the photographer play with his craft and his art. They both need to support one another. The photographer should try to understand and solve the problems the art director has.

L.A.: Have you known ideal collaborations like that?

Bob Miller: Yes. I have been very lucky and worked with some great art directors who let me do what I wanted 90% of the time. One example was on a shoot for Volvo. The image was the car with a battleship behind. I suggested using a grey car and painting everything in the foreground grey including the people. The art director backed me all the way and the picture was great. It went on to win a photographic gold award. Another example was a series of period car shots for an insurance company. I suggested that we take the cars on location and include people. Again, the art director went along with the idea and we won an award for best b/w press campaign. It just goes to prove that, if the collaboration between art director and photographer is good, you can make the ad even better. One time, I was working with three art

Volvo ad shot by Bob Miller in 1987 for Abbott Mead Vickers, London. Headline: "Is this the first car with an anti-submarine device?"

Image from a Marlboro campaign shot by Bob Miller.

directors for two months on a shoot. Fortunately, they were all very talented and there were no problems. It was amusing, however, when we were looking for locations together because we all had cameras round our necks so no one knew who the photographer was. I've found that, in the past, art directors supported photographers a lot more than they do today. Nowadays, everyone wants to know and see what the photograph is going to be like before it's even taken.

L.A.: Why is it that, sometimes, photographers don't always produce their best work in an advertising context?

Bob Miller: Reportage photographers don't generally do great advertising work. This type of photography is really difficult to control. They're on their own, they're working on a story, they have to react quickly – and so they're not used to being art-directed. Plus, the brief is generally nothing like the subject matter they usually photograph. The other sort of photographer who will suffer is the one who has a very strong personal look. It's difficult to compromise this type of work and, if you do, you lose its very essence. A talented commercial photographer will take an idea on board and bend it to their way of seeing.

L.A.: You have worked in rather different fields of photography, right? A wide variety of subject matters?

Bob Miller: I love all the different fields of photography – portraits, landscapes, reportage, nudes. And I've been very fortunate that art directors have used me for a wide variety of subject matters. At the same time, it has made it harder for me to make my mark because I haven't concentrated on any one aspect. A friend of mine only uses a 10x8 camera, so when you look at his work you can see a similarity of style running through it. But I love all cameras and the different things that they can do. I want to play with my art, and restricting myself to one area just wouldn't

suit me. It usually starts with a project, and the project usually leads me to a certain camera. I use my 35mm like a sketchbook; it keeps me looking and studying. A 5x4 forces you into deciding where to place the camera and gives you great quality. At the moment, I'm doing a series of photographs on smokers called The Cigarette Lepers. This involves working quickly to capture an image, so I'm tackling the project in a reportage way and using my Leica M6. One of my past projects was about my local area. I used to walk my dog every day across Putney Common and along the River Thames, and I wanted to capture the size of the landscapes. But the camera had to be handheld because of the nature of my walk, so the camera I used was a Linhof 6x12. Photographing people is the best – finding out about the person, trying to create an image that says something about the sitter. I'm in the middle of a project on Grand Chessmasters, which I'm doing in collaboration with an artist friend of mine called Barry Martin. Originally, the idea was that he would paint on top of my print, adding another layer to the image, but so far he has chosen not to alter any of my images and just added a tiny, hidden chess piece. For this project, I'm using an old Hasselblad and a P45 digital back.

L.A.: What would you say were the highlights of your career?

Bob Miller: Whenever someone has bought one of my photographs. Whenever I won an award. Whenever I was given a campaign that had a lot of potential. And whenever I took a great image.

L.A.: What are the most striking trends in photography of the past few years?

Bob Miller: Unfortunately, photography has become illustrative. With photographers now able to use Photoshop so well, photography has lost its credibility. There is no longer a truth about the photographic image. Portraits are so retouched and enhanced they have no feeling. You can see every detail in an image but they can lack any mood. Digitization and Photoshop are great tools but they need to be handled with care.

L.A.: You're one of the founders of Lensmodern, which has Sir John Hegarty on its board of directors. Can you tell us what

made you decide to found a company that is different from the usual image banks?

Bob Miller: The idea of Lensmodern was suggested by a friend more than eight years ago after I told him about a recent trip to America. Visiting ad agencies, I had observed that they were using stock photography for presentation layouts so that the client no longer had to approve rough drawings but was being shown something that resembled a finished ad. From this, I developed the concept of a high-quality stock library that could provide inspirational photography not only for layouts but also for the actual ads themselves. I felt that such a company could cover other areas as well, such as the selling of fine art prints and displaying of commercial portfolios, both of which are now incorporated on our site. I had never wanted my images to be with any of the existing commercial stock libraries, and I knew there were a lot of top creative photographers who felt like me. I wanted to form a company with quality photography as its core ethos. But it also had to be a company that was run by photographers, with fair, photographer-friendly contracts and the best interests of photographers at heart. Max Forsythe and Rolph Gobits joined me as directors and we now have nearly two hundred world-class photographers on board. Four years on from our commercial launch, I believe we offer one of the best and most unique collections of photographs available on the internet. Our online gallery includes many previously unseen images from our photographers' personal archives. Our board of directors has increased and John Hegarty has become our chairman. We've had shows in five London advertising agencies and held our first Lensmodern exhibition at the Daylight Zone studio in Peckham last December. We have many more plans for the future, including the introduction of a Lensmodern film stock section, a series of masterclasses featuring Lensmodern photographers, and the production of several promotional films on individual members that will be circulated to agencies and design groups in particular.

L.A.: Can you think of a recent photographic image – good or bad – that has struck you in an extraordinary fashion?

Bob Miller: I love the images of a photographer called Gregory Crewdson, whose work is storytelling – big productions, great lighting and attention to detail in regard to props and wardrobe. I would have loved to have done some of his photographs.

⌂: Joan Garrigosa ⌂: FP7, Dubai ⌂: Maged Nassar, Fadi Yaish ⌂: Vileda

: Joan Garrigosa : Bassat Ogilvy, Barcelona : TMB

📷: Adam Taylor ⌒: JWT, Sydney ⎘: John Lam, Andy Dilallo, Jay Benjamin ♔: Olympus

: Ross Brown ⌂: Publicis Mojo, Auckland ➯: Clara McLaurin ♕: Lion Nathan

📷: Sean Izzard ⌒: JWT, Sydney ▭►: John Lam ▽: Olympus

📷: Chris Frazer Smith ⌂: JWT, London ⌒: Rob Spicer ♕: HSBC

📷: Keisuke Kazui ⌂: Hakuhodo, Tokyo 🔊: Ryou Teshima 👑: MUFG

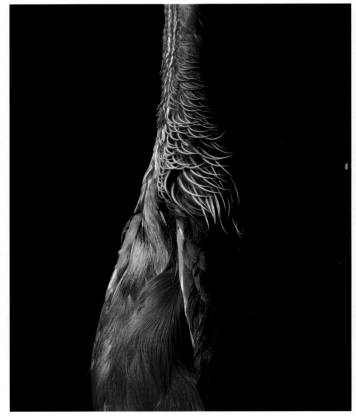

📷: Mark Laita 👑: Self-promotion

📷: Keisuke Kazui ⌂: Frontage, Tokyo ▭: Junji Fujimori ♔: BMW

📷: Jeremy Wong ⌂: Lowe, Jakarta ✏: Andruya Andrus ♔: Lifebuoy

◌: Lars Topelmann ♡: Self-promotion

⬡: Alex Telfer ♕: Self-promotion

⬡: Guy Neveling ⌂: JWT, London ▭: Royden Turner ♕: Cotonelle

📷: Cormac Hanley 👑: Self-promotion

📷: Takahito Sato ✍: McCann Erickson, Tokyo 🗂: Takayuki Nagai 👑: KIWI

📷: James Day 👑: Self-promotion

📷: Todd Antony 👑: Self-promotion

📷: Tom Nagy ⌂: The Gate Worldwide, Dusseldorf ▭: Bill Schwab ✎: Recom ♕: State Street

37

📷: Ross Brown ⌂: Saatchi & Saatchi, Wellington 🖴: Kate Dombroski ♕: Wellington Zoo

📷: Linda Jansen ✒: Paul Roberts ♕: WWF

📷: Markku Lahdesmaki 🅰: M&C Saatchi, Los Angeles 🖊: Sean Ohlenkamp 👑: San Diego Zoo

📷: Simon Harsent ⌂: Leo Burnett, Sydney ▭: Kieran Antill, Michael Canning ✎: Cream ♕: WWF

41

⬡: Staudinger+Franke ⌂: JWT, Dubai ⬜▸: Husen Baba ⩗: Greenpeace

📷: Bryan Traylor 🏠: Lowe Bull, Cape Town 🔦: Tariq Bailey, Cameron Watson 👑: Anti Animal Cruelty League

📷: Emir Haveric 👑: Self-promotion

📷: Antti Viitala 👑: Self-promotion

📷: Julien Vonier ⌂: Advico Young & Rubicam, Zurich ♛: Zoo Zurich

200bph 10.031

📷: Thomas von Salomon 👑: Self-promotion

📷: Steve Bonini 👑: Self-promotion

📷: Bryan Traylor ⌂: FoxP2, Cape Town 🔌: Ryan Barkhausen 👑: Master Lock

📷: Till Leeser ⌂: Töpfer, Grenville, Crone, Hamburg 👑: Papierunion

📷: Peter Yang 👑: Texas Monthly

: Paolo Marchesi ♕: Outdoor Life

: Zona13 ∩: Ogilvy & Mather, Milan ♕: Enpa

📷: Carlos Spottorno ⌂: DDB, Madrid ♕: Canary Islands Tourism Council

200bph 10.037

📷: Fernando Pellizzaro 👑: Self-promotion

📷: Carolina Simões Fernandes 👑: Self-promotion

📷: Mathias Baumann ⌂: Serviceplan, Dusseldorf ✏: Christoph Everke 👑: O2

📷: Christian Schmidt ⌂: Draftfcb, Hamburg ✏: Michael Thobe 👑: ABN Amro / RBS

📷: Egon Gade ♔: Self-promotion

📷: Christoph Morlinghaus ⌂: Victor Anselmi Studio, New York ♔: The Donaldson Organization

📷: Sharad Haksar ⌂: Cartwheel, Chennai, India 👑: Reliance Mobiles

📷: Christoph Morlinghaus 👑: Self-promotion

📷: Christoph Morlinghaus ⌂: Victor Anselmi Studio, New York 👑: The Donaldson Organization

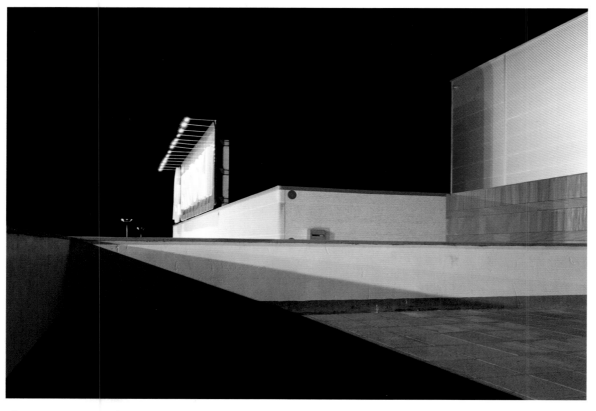

📷: Kai-Uwe Gundlach 👑: Self-promotion

📷: Frank Meyl 👑: AP25 American Photography Book

📷: Frank Meyl 👑: Milwaukee Art Museum

📷: Frank Meyl 👑: AP25 American Photography Book

📷: Frank Meyl ☖: Picture Magazine

📷: Ezra Gozo Mansur 📷➤: Cindy Goldstein 👑: Self-promotion

📷: Christoph Morlinghaus ♔: Wallpaper Magazine

📷: Frank Meyl ♔: Self-promotion

📷: Robert Tran 👑: Self-promotion

📷: Egon Gade 👑: Self-promotion

📷: Simon Stock 👑: Self-promotion

📷: Chris Frazer Smith ⌂: JWT, New York ✏: Brian Carley 👑: Jet Blue Airlines

📷: Julian Calverley ⌂: Brahm, Leeds 💬: Mike Thompson ♔: NDA

📷: Chris Frazer Smith ⌂: JWT, London ▭: Mark Norcutt ♡: HSBC

◻: Frank Schott ⌂: Goodby, Silverstein & Partners, San Francisco ▭: Croix Gagnon ♕: Hewlett Packard

📷: Simon Stock ⌂: Coast, London 👑: Toyota

📷: Simon Stock ♕: Volvo Magazine

: Martin Sigal ⌒: JWT, Buenos Aires ▭: Gonzalo Vecino, Miguel Usandivaras ♛: Ford

📷: Edo Kars ⌂: Ramp, Stuttgart ▭▶: Michael Köckritz 👑: Lamborghini

📷: Mats Cordt ⌂: Serviceplan, Munich 🖃: Matthias Harbeck ♛: BMW

: Steffen Schrägle : Self-promotion

: Steffen Schrägle : recom, Stuttgart : Porsche

⬚: Guy Farrow ⌂: Turnkey, Leeds ⬛: Richard Colvill ♛: Porsche

⬚: Steffen Schrägle ⌂: Creapress/BBDO, Paris ⬛: Nicolas Le Moing ♛: Nissan

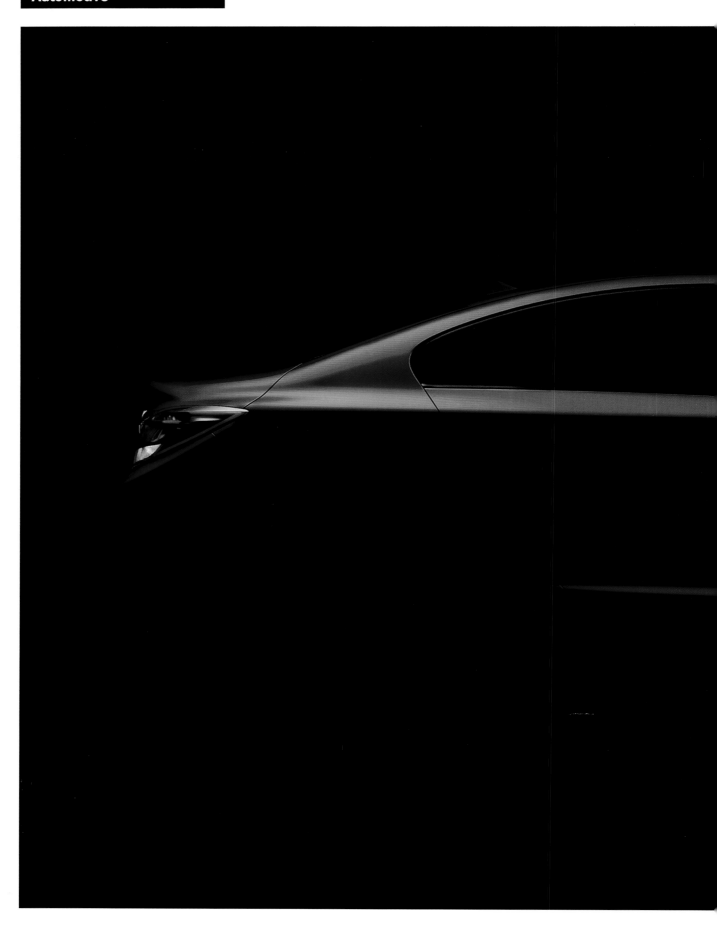

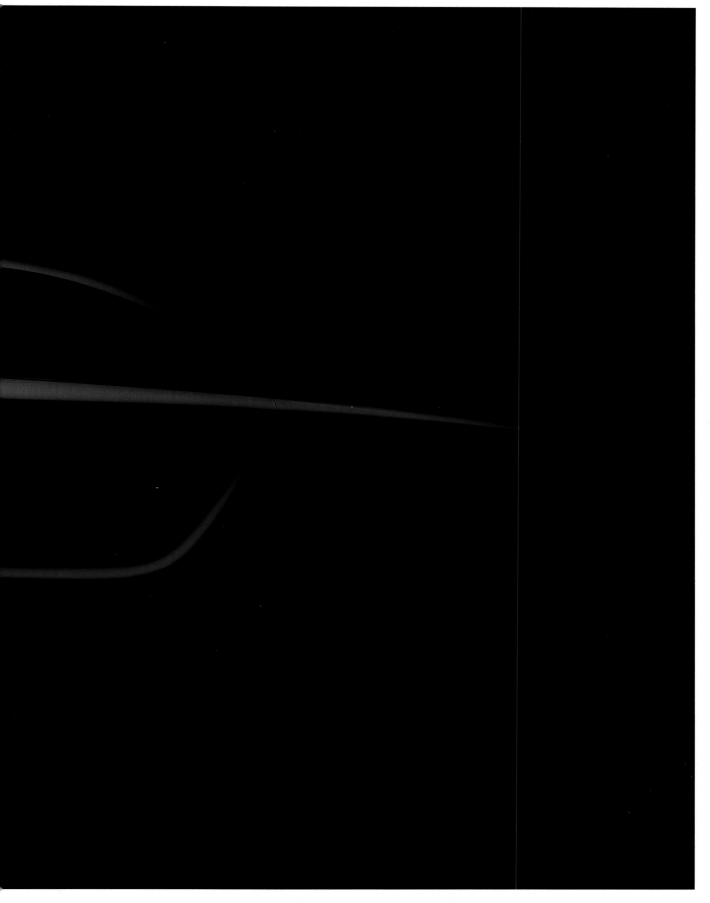

📷: RJ Muna ⌂: TBWA\Chiat\Day, Los Angeles ▭: Sheila Sullivan ♕: Infiniti – 2008 Pebble Beach Concours d'Elegance

◻: Vikram Bawa ▭: Vikram Bawa ♕: Skoda

◻: Bryan Helm ⌂: Data Armada, New York ▭: Reilly Saso, Bryan Helm ♕: Relish

: OliverStefan Photographers ᴀ: Crispin, Porter & Bogusky, Boulder, Colorado ᴡ: Volkswagen

📷: James Day ⌂: BBH, London ♕: Audi

📷: David de Jong ♕: Pelican Magazines Hearst

📷: Uwe Düttmann ⌒: Jung von Matt/Neckar, Stuttgart ▭: Tobias Eichinger ♔: Mercedes-Benz

: Thomas L. Fischer ⌂: Blösch & Partner, Eppingen, Germany ♛: Loctite

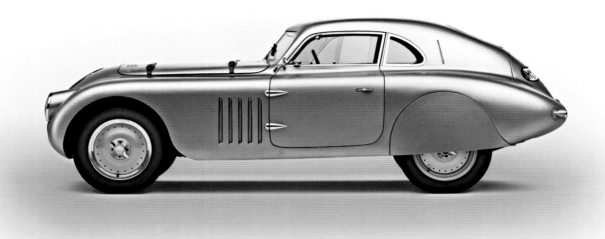

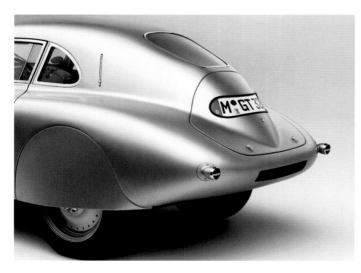

: Tif Hunter : Conran Octopus

📷: Frank Meyl 👑: PX3 Book

📷: Kevin Necessary ⌂: Siltanen and Partners, El Segundo, California ▭: John Payne ♛: Suzuki

📷: Ivo von Renner ⌂: WE Marketing, Bejing ♕: Mercedes-Benz

📷: William Huber ⌂: Von Gruber, London ▭: Jared Leeds ♕: Citroën

📷: Emir Haveric ☝: MAB, Berlin ▭►: Kai Grützmacher, Caroline Jacob ♛: BMW

📷: Alexandre Salgado ☝: Y&R, São Paulo ▭►: Axel Levay, Leandro Hermann ♛: LG

📷: Thomas von Salomon ⌒: Publicis, Paris ♕: Renault

📷: Daniel Hartz 🏠: Dentsu, Brussels 🖱: Benoit Lamy 👑: Lexus

: Caesar Lima : Self-promotion

📷: Thomas Smetana ⌂: Concepta, Steyr, Austria 🖊: Manfred Pfandlbauer ✎: Alexander Wilhelm 👑: Hammerer Aluminium Industries

📷: William So Yuen Kwok 🖊: William Chan Kwok Yee 👑: Elle Magazine

📷: Christophe Gilbert ⌒: Euro RSCG, Brussels ♛: Inno

📷: Christophe Gilbert ⌂: Adopt, Brussels 👄: Phil Vanduynen, Claudine Mergaerts 👑: Bogh-Art

: Caesar Lima ⬜: Neil Vilppu ⬥: Marzocchi

SHINE ON.

: Connie Hong : Grey, Hong Kong : Doris Leung : Pantene

: Basil Childers ᴀ: Lowe, Bangkok ⌐: Anan Nunsai ✐: Thanawat Hora (Undo) ♔: Exact Pregnancy Test

📷: Chico Audi ⌂: WF Propaganda, São Paulo 🖚: Zanchi Franco ♛: Forum

📷: Kurt Stallaert ⌂: TBWA, Brussels ▭: Alex Ameye ♛: Levis

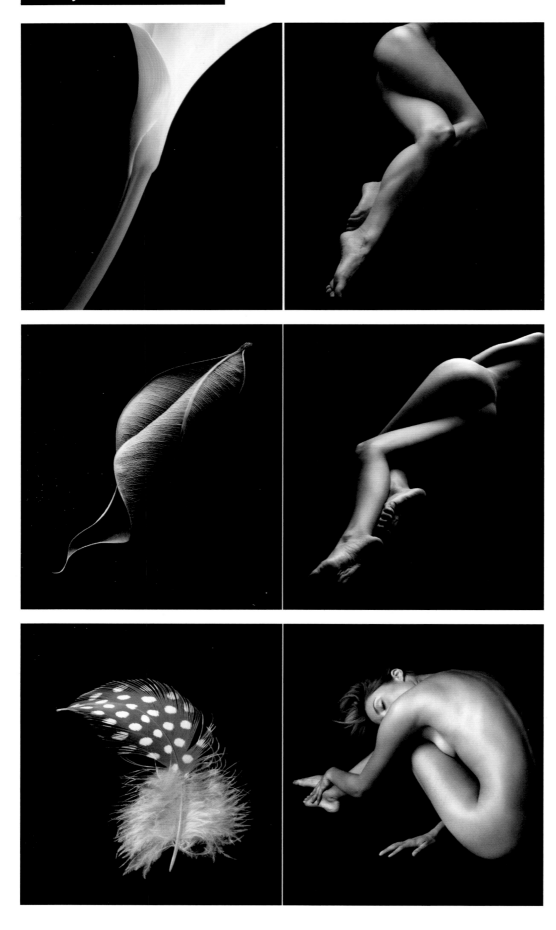

: Mark Laita 👑: Self-promotion

⬚: Eryk Fitkau ▭⊃: Eryk Fitkau ♛: Hair Backstage

⬚: Eryk Fitkau ⌂: The Gang, Singapore ▭⊃ Richard Johnson ♛: LaSalle College of the Art Singapore

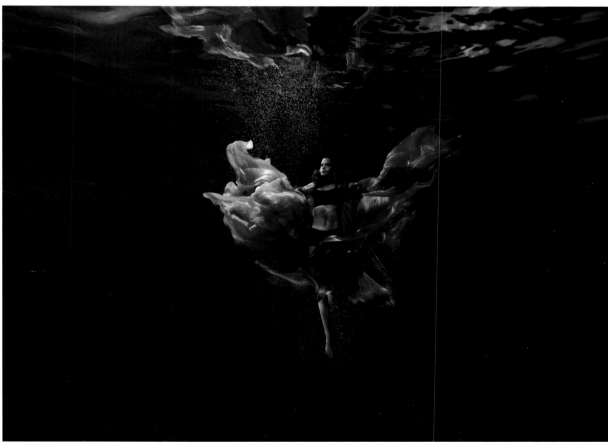

: Martin Sigal ⌒: BBDO, Buenos Aires ⌗: Gustavo Chiocconi ⌣: Propel

: RJ Muna : ODC/Dance

📷: Connie Hong 🅰: Ogilvy & Mather, Hong Kong 🖎: Joseph Wong 👑: Motorola

📷: Jonathan Knowles 👑: Luxure Magazine

📷: Connie Hong 🅰: Grey, Hong Kong 🖎: Doris Leung 👑: Cover Girl

⌓: Carlo Vigni ⌂: Catoni Associati, Florence ♕: Self-promotion

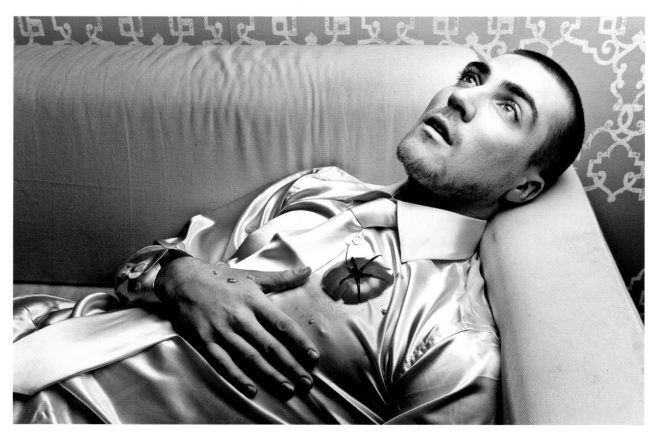

⌓: Cormac Hanley ♕: Self-promotion

📷: Connie Hong ⌂: Leo Burnett, Guanghzou, China 🍾: Liu Gang 👑: Anchor Beer

📷: Dustin Humphrey / Nouvelle Vague 👑: Surfing Magazine

📷: Carioca 🔨: BBDO, Moscow 👑: Eclipse

📷: Jatin Kampani 📷: Jatin Kampani 👑: Tarana Masand

📷: Ilan Hamra 👑: Vision Magazine

: Mark Westerby ⌂: Alcazar, Newcastle ▭: Antonio Bachini ♔: Princesshay

📷: Julia Fullerton-Batten ⌂: DDB, Warsaw 🖒: Nobodys Children Foundation

📷: Anders Hald 👑: Petit by Sofie Schnoor

📷: Anders Hald 👑: Exhibition Project Tarot

📷: Anders Hald 👑: Self-promotion

📷: Invy Ng ⌂: Bates 141, Ho Chi Minh City 🖊: John Sampson, Handri Ka ♛: Perfetti Van Melle

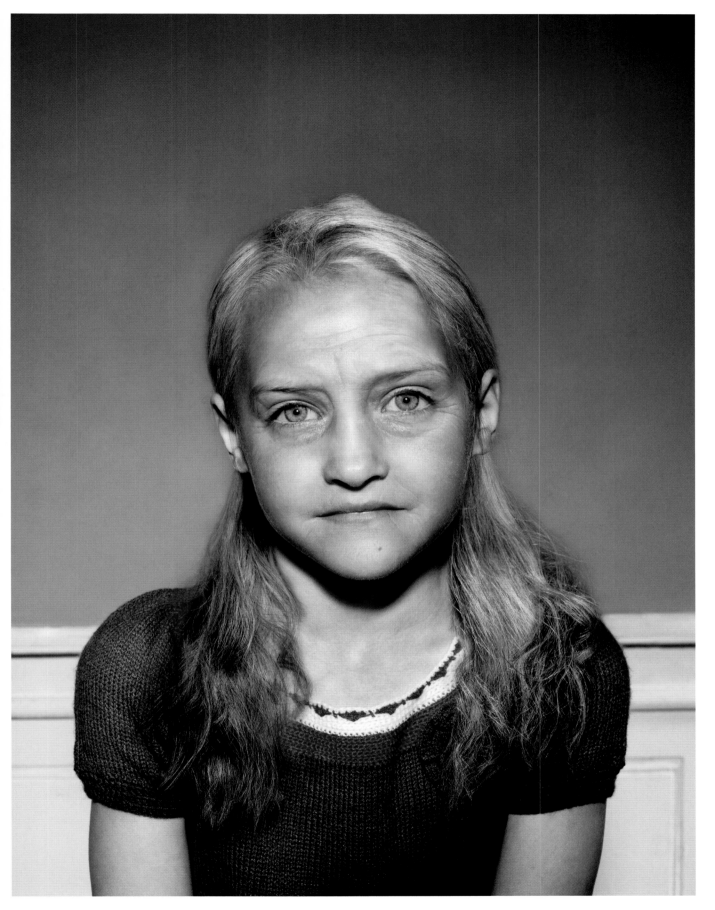

📷: Alex Telfer ⌂: M&C Saatchi, Paris ✏: Antoine Barthuel, Daniel Fohr, Caroline Picard ♕: Enfance et Partage

: Kelvin Murray ⌂: CHI & Partners, London ♡: Roy Castle Anti Smoking Trust

📷: Christophe Gilbert ⌂: Happiness, Brussels 🖊: Gregory Titeca ♛: Bellerose

📷: Jonathan Tay ⌂: JWT, Shanghai 👑: Cemal Cemil Bubble Gum Store

📷: Guy Farrow ⌒: McCann Erickson, Manchester ▭➤: Dave Eyre, Clive Davis ♈: Oilatum

: Guy Farrow : Self-promotion

📷: Scott A. Woodward ⌂: Lowe & Partners, Singapore ▭▷: Steve Straw ♕: The Emerging Lens Initiative

: Shin Sugino : Applied Arts Calendar

: Scott A. Woodward : Lowe & Partners, Singapore : Steve Straw : The Emerging Lens Initiative

📷: Beatrice Heydiri ⌒: Scholz & Friends, Berlin ♔: Bob Schokoladen Zigaretten

📷: Beatrice Heydiri ♔: Self-promotion

📷: Beatrice Heydiri 👑: Collezioni

📷: Edo Kars ⌂: Saatchi & Saatchi, Amsterdam 🖊: Nils Taildeman, Magnus Olsson 👑: Bambix

📷: Ezra Gozo Mansur 🔖: Yael L. Brandt 👑: Self-promotion

📷: Chico Audi 🔖: Igor Valverde 👑: Abrale

📷: Guy Neveling ⌂: Ogilvy, Cape Town ▭: Wallace Seggie ♛: Volkswagen

📷: the unknown artist ♛: H Magazine

📷: Sharad Haksar 👑: Self-promotion

📷: Jamie MacFadyen ⌂: M&C Saatchi, Sydney ▭: Michael Andrews ♔: Woolworth

📷: Joshua Dalsimer ⌂: Mother, London ✏: Peter Robertson ♛: Diet Coke

📷: Ira Bordo 👑: Venera Kazarova

📷: Alexandra Zakharova & Ilya Plotnikov 👑: Self-promotion

⬡: James Day ♡: Self-promotion

[Camera]: Connie Hong [Person]: TBWA, Hong Kong [Clothing]: Tony Tsang, Flora Tsui [Crown]: Harvey Nichols

📷: Adrian Cook ⌂: M&C Saatchi, Sydney ♔: British Council

📷: RJ Muna ♔: La Pocha Nostra

📷: Vikram Bawa ⌃: P9, Mumbai ▭: Kannani Paras ♛: Catwalk

📷: Erik Almas ▭: Stephen Kamifuji ⚗: Erik Almas ♛: Genlux

📷: Paul Ruigrok ⌂: TBWA\PHS, Helsinki 📷: Paula Orre 🖌: Fisk-Imaging ♔: DNA

: David Sykes : Self-promotion

:camera: David Sykes :crown: Self-promotion

📷 : Jason Hindley 👑 : Self-promotion

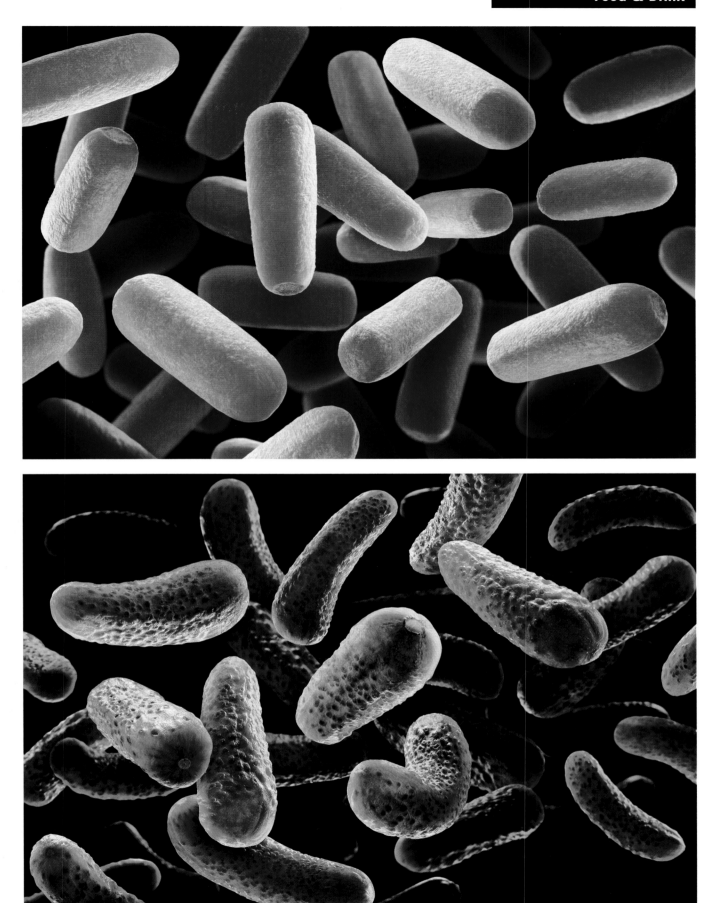

: StudioMe : DCS, Porto Alegre, Brazil : Maurício Oliveira, Vinicius Turani : Tramontina

: Dan Goldberg : Self-promotion

📷: Jürgen Schwope 🏵: Self-promotion

: Josh Wood ⌂: McCann Erickson, Salt Lake City ▭: Phil Hunter ♛: Nature's Products

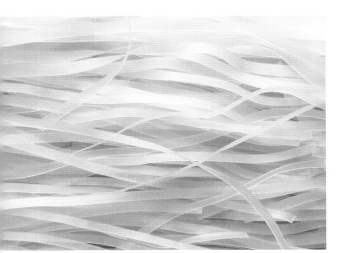

: Beth Galton ♛: Self-promotion

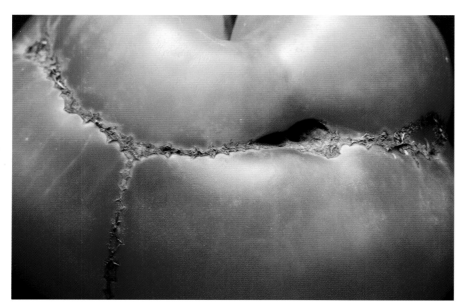

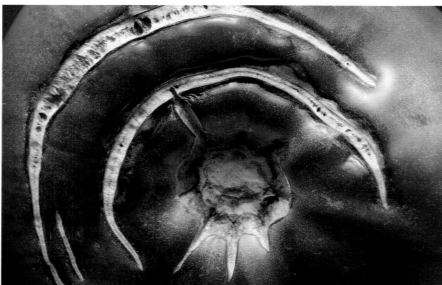

: Beth Galton : Self-promotion

📷: Nadav Kander ⌂: Droga5, New York 🔋: January Vernon 👑: Puma

📷: David Sykes ⌂: AMV BBDO, London ✏: Pete Davies ♕: Heinz

📷: Christoph Morlinghaus 👑: Wallpaper Magazine

📷: Michael Schnabel 👑: Zeit Magazin

📷: Sharad Haksar ⌂: 1pointsize, Chennai, India ♔: Stori

📷: Kelvin Murray ⌂: CHI & Partners, London ♛: Big Yellow

📷: Peter Leverman 👕: Self-promotion

📷: Julian Calverley ♔: Self-promotion

📷: Mats Cordt ♔: Self-promotion

📷: Christian Schmidt ⌂: Cline Davis & Mann, New York ▭►: Lou Massaia ♔: Sutent

📷: Richard Schultz ♔: Harper Collins Publishers

: Alex Telfer ⌂: M&C Saatchi, London ▭: Tiger Savage ♔: Royal Bank of Scotland

: Alex Telfer ♔: Self-promotion

: Ian Butterworth : Self-promotion

📷: Cameron Davidson 👑: Vanity Fair Magazine

📷: Christian Schmidt ⌂: Philipp und Keuntje, Hamburg ✏: Zoran Drobina, Oliver Zacharias-Tölle ♛: Deutsche Telekom

📷: Pete Seaward 👑: Lonely Planet

📷: Erik Chmil 👑: Self-promotion

: Cameron Davidson ♔: Self-promotion

: Alex Telfer ⌂: M&C Saatchi, London ▭: Tiger Savage ♔: Royal Bank of Scotland

: Ralph Baiker ⌂: BBDO, Dusseldorf ▭: Sven Klasen, Stephan Eichler ♡: Smart

🖭: Kai-Uwe Gundlach ⌂: Scholz & Friends, Berlin 🗩: Paul Fleig, Nurten Zeren ♕: DB Schenker

⬚: Staudinger+Franke ⌂: RKCR/Y&R, London ✏: Dan Hubert, Freddy Mandy ♔: Visit London

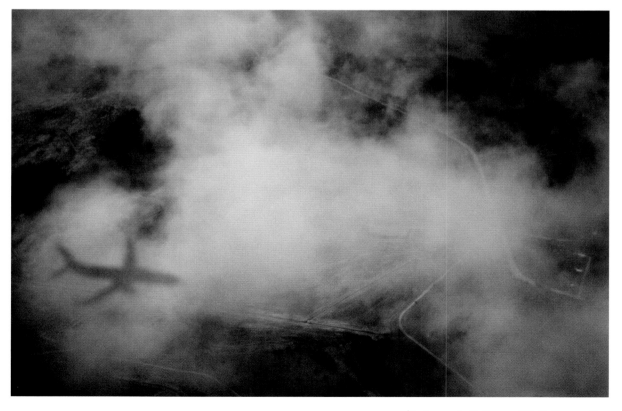

⬚: Fernando Pellizzaro ♔: Self-promotion

📷: Manu Agah ⌂: Saatchi & Saatchi Design, London ▭: Stuart Fuller ♕: Toyota

: Michael Schnabel : Self-promotion

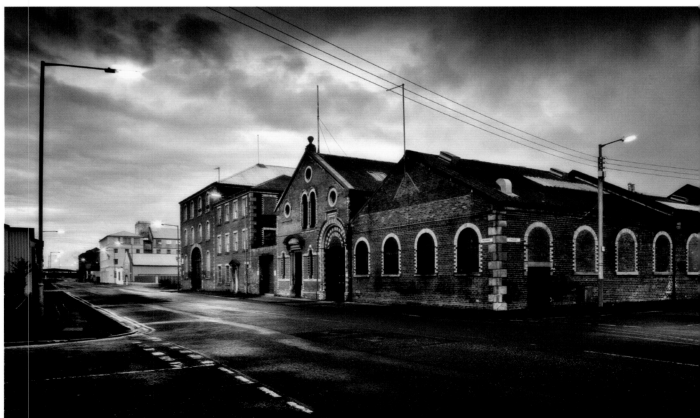

📷: Dirk Karsten 👑: Self-promotion

: Oscar van de Beek : Self-promotion

: Simon Harsent : Self-promotion

📷: Stan Musilek 👑: GEO Magazine

📷: Simon Harsent ⌒: Leo Burnett, Sydney ▭: Kieran Antill, Michael Canning 🖌: Cream ♡: WWF

📷: Steffen Schrägle ♡: Self-promotion

📷: Eliseo Miciu ♕: National Geographic

PHARES **MARCHAL** BOUGIES **MARCHAL**

📷: Steffen Schrägle ⌂: Creapress/BBDO, Paris 🗩: Nicolas Le Moing ⌣: Nissan

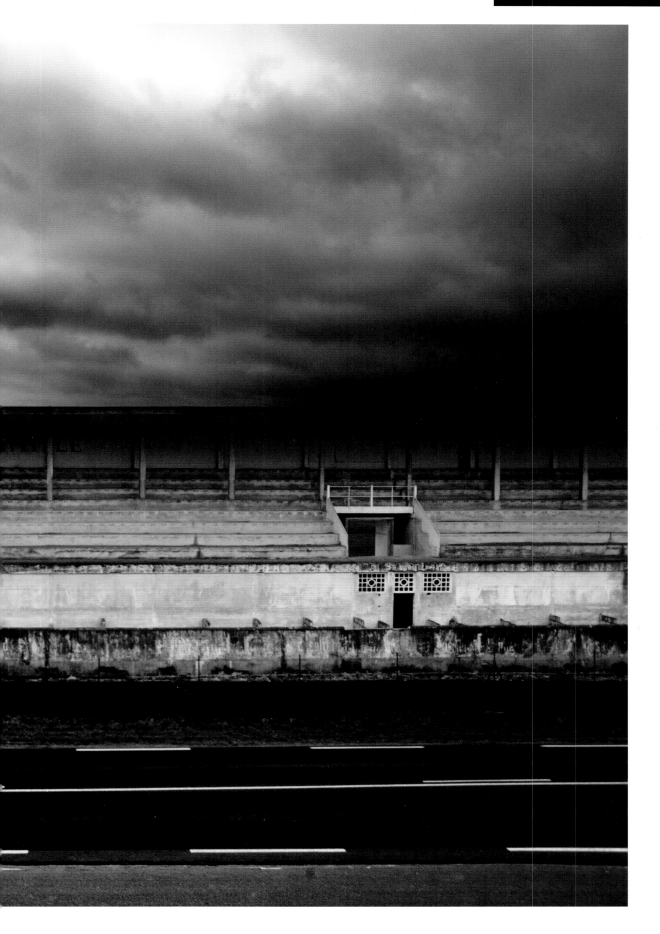

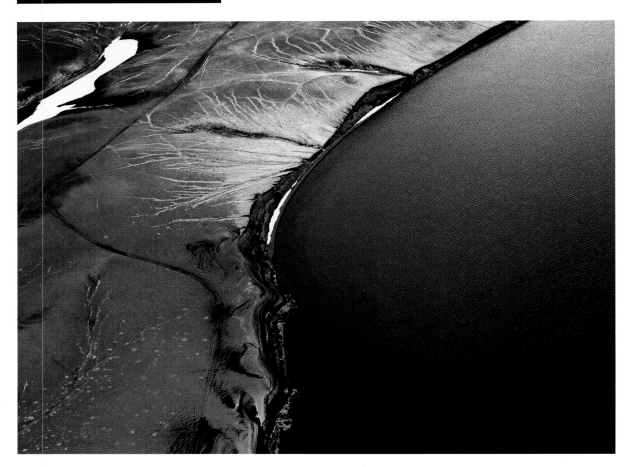

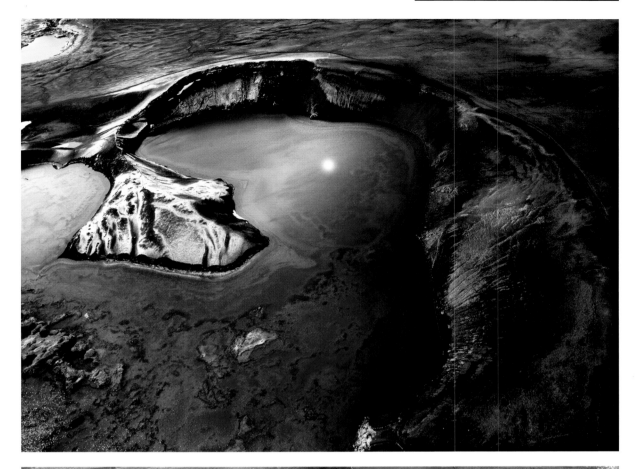

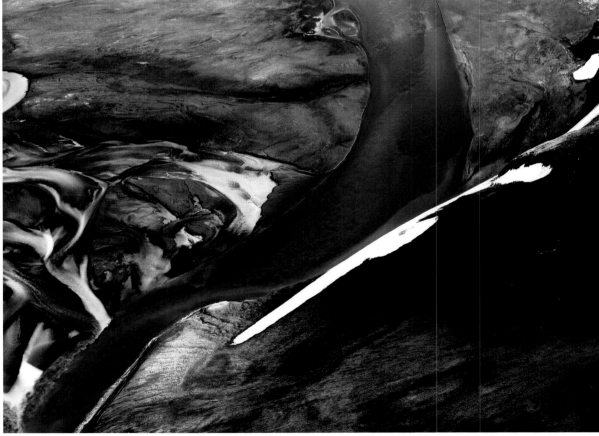

⌖: Stuart Hall ⌂: CSS Europe, Birmingham ♕: International Trucks

📷: Andreas Hempel ⊔: Self-promotion

◻: Julian Calverley ♕: Self-promotion

◻: Jean Marie Vives ⌂: Saatchi & Saatchi, Paris ▭: Emmanuelle Maliakas & Guillaume Fillion ♕: Toyota

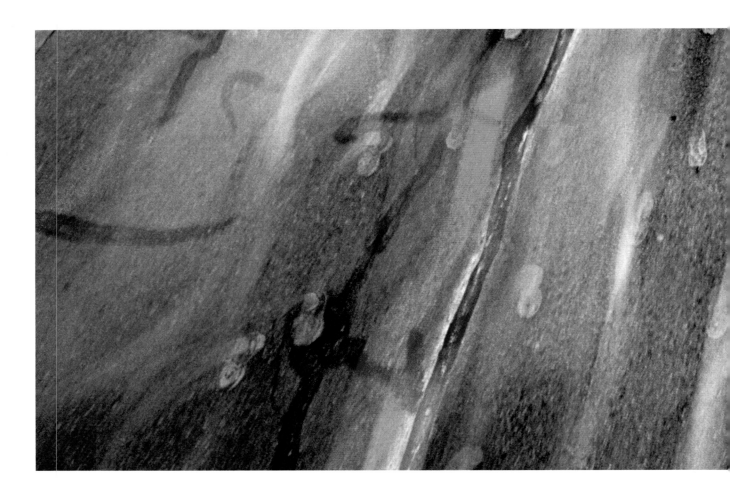

📷: Ivo von Renner ⌂: LässingMüller, Stuttgart ♔: Daimler

📷: Steven Wohlwender ⌂: Highland Group, Grand Rapids, Michigan ▭▷: Geoff Shirley ♔: Highland Group

📷: Robert Schlatter 🧺: Self-promotion

◻️: Erik Chmil ♔: Self-promotion

◻️: Sean Izzard ♔: Pool

📷: Christian Schmidt 👑: Self-promotion

📷: Steffen Schrägle 👑: Self-promotion

📷: Simon Harsent ♔: Self-promotion

📷: Julian Calverley ♔: Self-promotion

📷: Julian Calverley ♡: Self-promotion

📷: John Offenbach 👑: Self-promotion

📷: John Offenbach ♔: Self-promotion

📷: John Offenbach ♛: Self-promotion

📷: Ezra Gozo Mansur ▭▷: Ezra Gozo Mansur ♛: Self-promotion

📷: Mark Westerby ⌂: Twentyseven, Newcastle ▭▸: Richard Fowler ♛: Cleveland Council

📷: Chico Audi 🖱: Anders Serra 👑: HBO

📷: Simon Stock ♕: Self-promotion

[camera]: Mathias Baumann [crown]: Self-promotion

[camera]: Julian Calverley [crown]: Self-promotion

📷: Dirk Karsten 👑: Self-promotion

📷: Paolo Marchesi ♔: Outside Magazine

📷: Chico Audi ▭: Marcio Olyntho ♔: Fine Art

📷: Eliseo Miciu ♕: Self-promotion

📷: Robert Tran ♕: Self-promotion

📷: William Huber 🔲: Sean Austin, Rudi Anggono 👑: Self-promotion

📷: Robert Tran 👑: Self-promotion

📷: Christian Schmidt 👑: Self-promotion

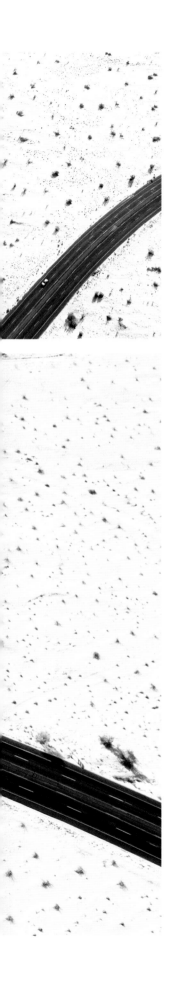

: Oscar van de Beek ⌣: Self-promotion

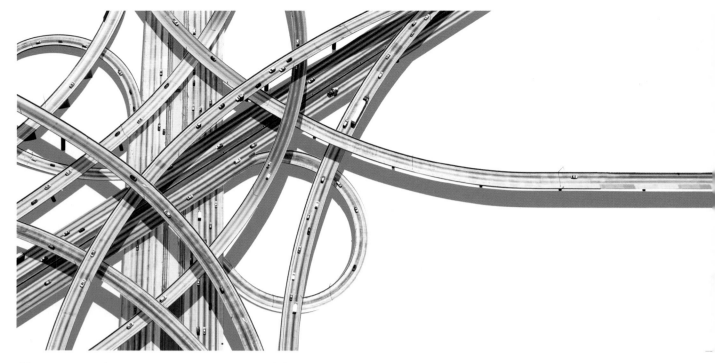

📷: Simon Stock ⌂: Hamon Associates, Los Angeles ♔: Hyundai

📷: Jean Marie Vives ⌂: BETC Euro RSCG, Paris ▭▸: Helen Ortiz ♔: Veolia Environment

📷: Jonathan May ⌂: Thread Creative, Sydney ▭➤: Jonathan Palasty 👑: Broadway Gym

📷: Martin Schoeller 👑: GQ

📷: Martin Schoeller 👑: Rolling Stone Magazine

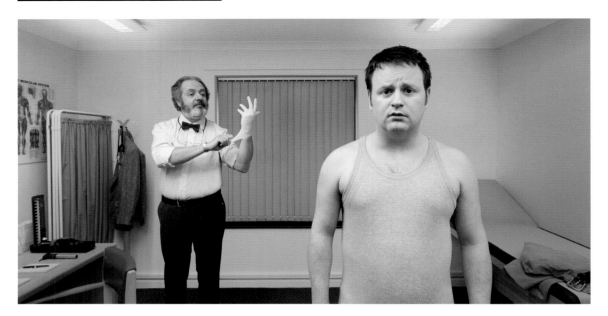

📷: David Stewart ☌: Kindred, London ▭▷: Simon Brotherson ♛: Wells and Young

📷: David Stewart ▭: Mohamed Bareche ♔: Self-promotion

📷: Johann Sebastian Hänel ⌒: Kakoii, Berlin ♔: Stephanus Stiftung

📷: StudioMe ⌂: DCS, Porto Alegre, Brazil 📇: Gregory Kickow 👑: MARGS

: Guy Neveling ⌂: Ogilvy, Cape Town ⊏⊐: Jamie Mietz ♔: The Times

241   200bph 10.008

📷: Ionut Macri 🎨: Alex Deaconu 👑: The One Magazine

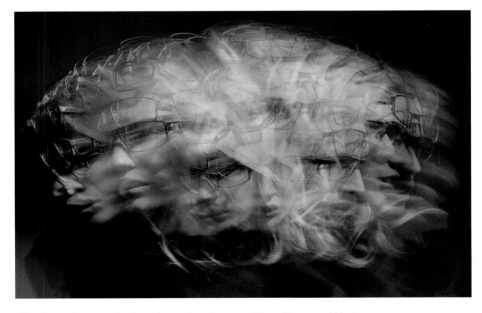

⬡: Klaus Thymann ⌂: Squash'em, London ⎙: Klaus Thymann ♛: Orgreen

📷: Joseph Ford 🏠: BETC Euro RSCG, Paris 🗔: Viken Guzel 👑: Disneyland Paris

📷: Ricardo Barcellos ⌂: Ogilvy, São Paulo ♕: Coca-Cola

📷: Uwe Düttmann ⌂: Kempertrautmann, Hamburg ✏: Frank Bannöhr ♕: Audi

📷: Cormac Hanley ♕: Self-promotion

📷: Sven Glage ⌂: Kolle Rebbe, Hamburg 🖊: Alexander Hesslein ♕: Readybank

📷: Sven Glage ⌂: Jung von Matt, Berlin 🖊: Daniel Haschtmann ♕: 13th Street TV-Channel

📷: Anthony Redpath ⌂: Publicis, Vancouver ♛: Burnaby Tourism

📷: Peter Yang ♛: Boost Mobile

📷: Michael Muller 👑: Trauma

📷: Michael Muller 👑: Von Zipper

⌖: Dustin Humphrey / Nouvelle Vague ♕: Insight

📷: Thomas Chadwick ⌒: Y&R, Chicago ▭⊃: Chris von Ende ♛: Companions for Seniors

📷: Tony Garcia 👑: Self-promotion

📷: Stewart Charles Cohen 🏢: Red7e, Louisville, Kentucky 🖊: Dan Barbercheck 👑: Baptist Hospital East

📷: Staudinger+Franke 📷: Andreas Franke 👑: Self-promotion

📷: Staudinger+Franke ⌂: Euro RSCG, Vienna ✏: Dan Hubert, Freddy Mandy
👑: Neunerhaus

: Hans Starck ⌂: JWT, New York ▭: Raphael Milczarek ♛: Visine

: Michael Meyersfeld ⟨⟩: Self-promotion

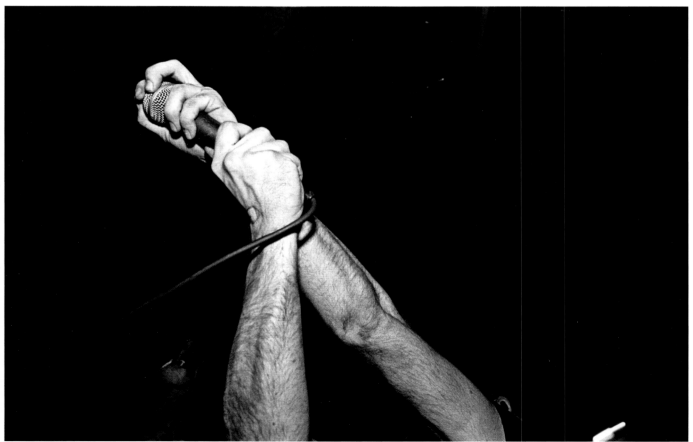

📷: Mark Murrmann ⌂: Energy BBDO, Chicago ▭: Jason Stanfield 👑: Jim Beam

📷: Shin Sugino 👑: Applied Arts Calendar

📷: Ilan Hamra 👑: Self-promotion

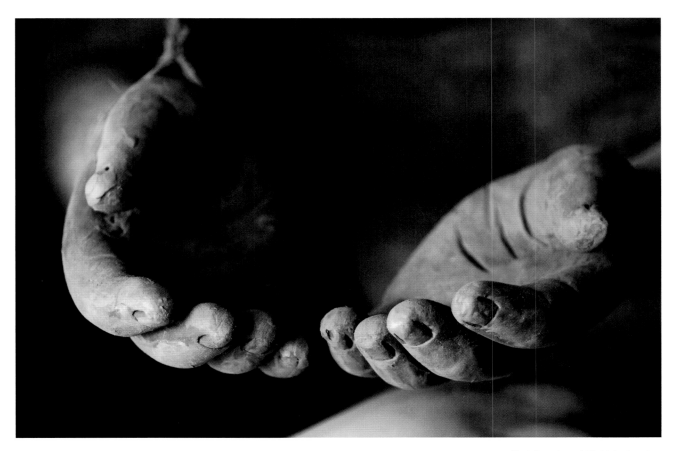

📷: Vikas Dutt 👑: Help Tourism

📷: Lyndon Wade ⌂: Grid, Johannesburg 🪄: realfake 👑: Virgin Mobile

📷: Mark Zibert 👑: Driven Magazine

: The Wade Brothers: David Lindsey Wade & Lyndon Wade ♔: WAD Magazine

: The Wade Brothers: David Lindsey Wade & Lyndon Wade ♔: FLY 53

📷: Lewis Ho ⌂: Leo Burnett, Hong Kong ▭: Kenny Ip, Jacky Tong ♔: Greenpeace

📷: Manoj Jadhav 📷▷: Manoj Jadhav 👑: Little Shilpa

📷: Mat Blamires ⌂: Clemenger BBDO, Wellington ✏: Paul Nagy, Paul Young, Brigid Alkema ♕: Land Transport NZ and NZ Police

📷: Steve Bonini ⌂: McKee Wallwork, Cleveland ▭: Pat Feehery, Bart Cleveland ♕: Slipstream Auto Care

📷: Matias Posti ⌂: Injaus, Buenos Aires ▭: Mariano Abad, Marcelo Virgillito ♕: Turner

📷: Jim Fiscus ▭▷: Jim Fiscus ♔: Self-promotion

📷: Rainer Stratmann ⌂: Alice BBDO, Istanbul ▭: Kutlay Sindirgi ♕: Mercedes-Benz

📷: William Huber ⌂: Eric Mower and Associates, Charlotte, North Carolina ▭: Patrick Short ♕: Nucor Steel Company

📷: Hans Starck ⌢: Scholz and Friends, Berlin ⌁: Matthias Spätgens, Matthias Rebmann ♛: Frankfurter Allgemeine Zeitung

📷: Julian Calverley ♛: Self-promotion

When everyday movements seem impossible.

When everyday movements seem impossible.

📷: Parker Biley Photography ⌂: Saatchi & Saatchi, Milan ♛: Voltaren

📷: William Huber 🅰: M&C Saatchi, Sydney 👑: Abu-Dhabi Tourism

📷: Vikas Dutt 👑: Help Tourism

📷: Stuart Hamilton 🏠: Euro RSCG, London 📇: Alexi Berwitz 👑: Airbus

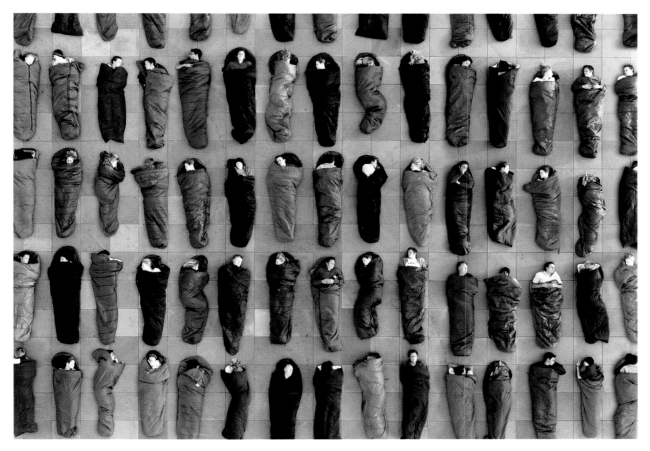

📷: Stuart Hamilton ⌒: TBWA, London ▭►: Steve Williams ♔: Sony Playstation

📷: Sandro ⌒: Ogilvy & Mather, Chicago ▭►: Gabe Usadel ♔: Chicago 2016 Olympic Proposal

📷: Randal Ford 🖍️: Marty Butler 🖌️: Portus Imaging 👑: Self-promotion

📷: Markku Lahdesmaki ⌂: ML Rogers, New York 📷: Brian Gibson ♔: Atlantis

📷: Anthony Redpath 👑: Self-promotion

⃝: Kai-Uwe Gundlach ⌃: Select NY, Berlin ⌷: Bernhard Schulze ⌣: Aktion Mensch –
Die Gesellschafter

📷: William Huber ▭▸: Sean Austin, Rudi Anggono ♕: Self-promotion

📷: Michael Corridore ⌂: BMF, Sydney ▭▸: Jake Rusznyak ♕: Schweppes

📷: Christian Schmidt ⌂: Ogilvy & Mather, Frankfurt am Main ✏: Irina Schestakoff, Christian Mommertz ♕: Siemens

📷: Pete Seaward ♕: Four Seasons Hotel & Resorts

📷: Mats Cordt ⌂: Kolle Rebbe, Hamburg 🖊: Rolf Leger 👑: ZDF

📷: Antti Viitala 👑: Self-promotion

📷: Pier Nicola D'Amico 👑: Self-promotion

📷: Adam Taylor ⌂: Ward 6, Sydney 📷▷: Grant Foster, Richard Price ♔: Bayer

📷: Shoda Masahiro ⌂: Senha&Co., Tokyo 👄: Chie Morimoto 👑: Toys Factory

📷: Steffen Schrägle 👑: Self-promotion

📷: Sandro 👑: Charta

📷: Mats Cordt 👑: Self-promotion

: Edo Kars ⌂: Tribal DDB, Amsterdam 🖇: Jean Pierre Kin, Chris Baylis, Neil Dawson ♛: Philips

: Florian Geiss : Self-promotion

📷: Florian Geiss 👑: Self-promotion

📷: Andy Glass ⌂: Y&R, Paris ♛: Nespresso

📷: Erik Almas ⌒: Glass McClure, Sacramento ▭▷: Jay F. Miller ♔: Amtrak

📷: Jaap Vliegenthart ⌒: McCann Erickson, Oslo ⎙: Geir Florhaug ✎: Rutger Luijs, Souverein ♕: Statoil Hydro

📷: Uwe Düttmann ⌒: Publicis, Zurich ⎙: Sascha Moser, Tim Hoppin ♕: Zürich Versicherung

: Chris Gordaneer ∩: DDB, Toronto ⊏⊐: Paul Wallace ♔: Bosch

📷: Normand Robert ⌃: Taxi, Montreal ▭: Jean-Luc Dion ♛: MSN

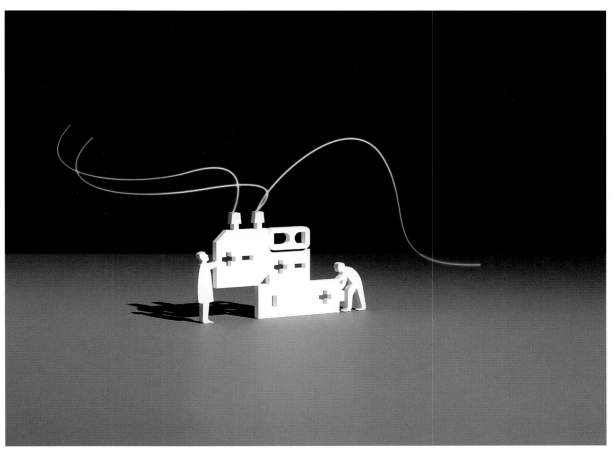

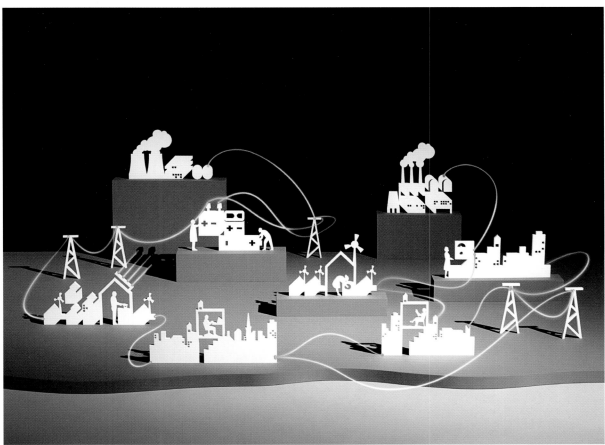

📷: James Day 👑: Wired Magazine

📷: Joshua Dalsimer ⌂: Mother, New York ▷: Mat Driscoll ♕: Dell

📷: James Day 👑: Self-promotion

📷: James Day 👑: Wired Magazine

📷: Teo Chai Guan ⌂: Saatchi & Saatchi, Singapore ♛: Lego

📷: Robert Schlatter 🖍: Dan Chau 👑: Neutrogena

📷: Jimmy Fok 🅰: Ogilvy & Mather, Singapore 👑: FHM

📷: Motoki Nihei ⌒: Fallon, Tokyo ▭▷: Keiichi Uemura ♔: Tokyo Institute of Art and Design

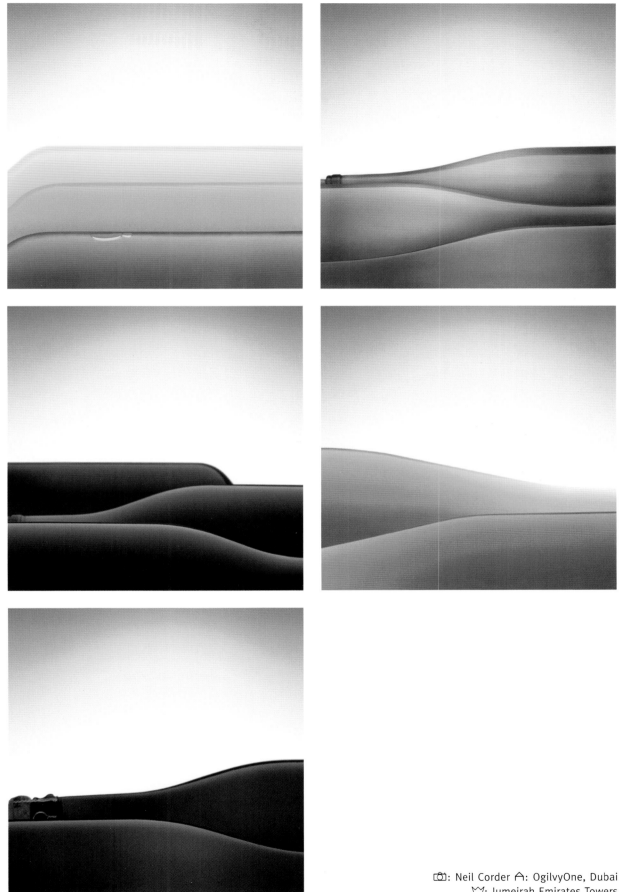

📷: Neil Corder ⌂: OgilvyOne, Dubai
♕: Jumeirah Emirates Towers

📷: Martin Sigal ⌂: Ponce, Buenos Aires 📷: Facundo Romero 👑: Axe

📷: Peter Yang 👑: Rolling Stone Magazine

: Simon Harsent ⌂: Three Drunk Monkeys, Sydney ▭: Matt Heck, Noah Regan ✎: Cream ♛: Unwired

: David Lindsey Wade ♛: Sound and Fury

📷: Chris Frazer Smith ✏: Stephen Parker 👑: Random House

📷: Shinji Watanabe 📷: Shinji Watanabe 🖌: Shinji Watanabe 👑: Bajra

📷: Uwe Düttmann ⌂: TBWA, Shanghai ▭: Johnson Sheng, Lesley Zhou ♛: adidas

📷: Uwe Düttmann ⌂: Jung von Matt/Neckar, Stuttgart ✏: Tobias Eichinger ♕: Mercedes-Benz

📷: Stefano Gilera ⌂: Mondadori, Milan ♛: Men's Health

📷: Kai-Uwe Gundlach ⌒: Ringzwei, Hamburg ▭: Dirk Linke ♛: BMW Magazine

📷: the unknown artist ♛: Chill Out Fashion

: Stuart Hall ⛑: Dunkin Design

📷: Stuart Hall 👑: Self-promotion

📷: Paul Ross Jones ⌂: Ilizz, Beijing ✏: Darryl Parsons 👑: 42 Below Vodka

📷: Dean Alexander 🔋: Ieva Katana 👑: Pastaiga Magazine

📷: Christian Schmidt ⌂: Draftfcb, Hamburg ✏: Michael Thobe 👑: ABN Amro / RBS

📷: Frank Meyl 👑: PX3 Book

📷: Boudewijn Smit ⌂: Instinct, Rome 👑: Mercedes-Benz

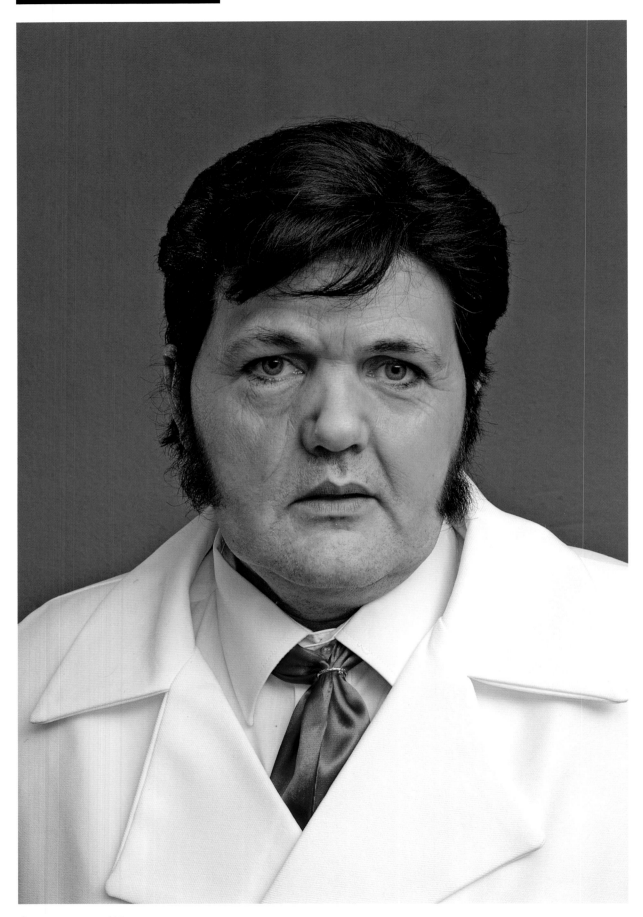

📷: Moritz Steiger 👑: Self-promotion

📷: Landry Major 🖊: Donovan Craig ✨: Stevie Verroca 👑: Fight! Magazine

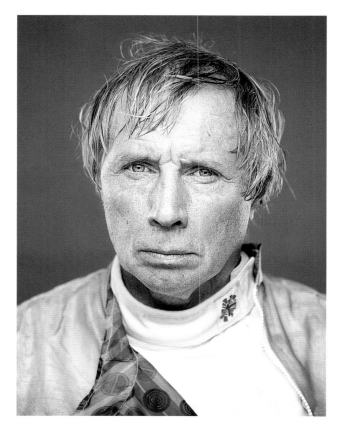

📷: Simon Stock 👑: Self-promotion

📷: Guy Farrow 🖊: Guy Farrow 👑: adidas

📷: James Day 👑: Audi Magazine

200bph 10.004

📷: Robert Wilson ✀: Leo Burnett, London ✏: Rob Tenconi ♔: NHS

📷: Robert Wilson ♔: Sunday Times

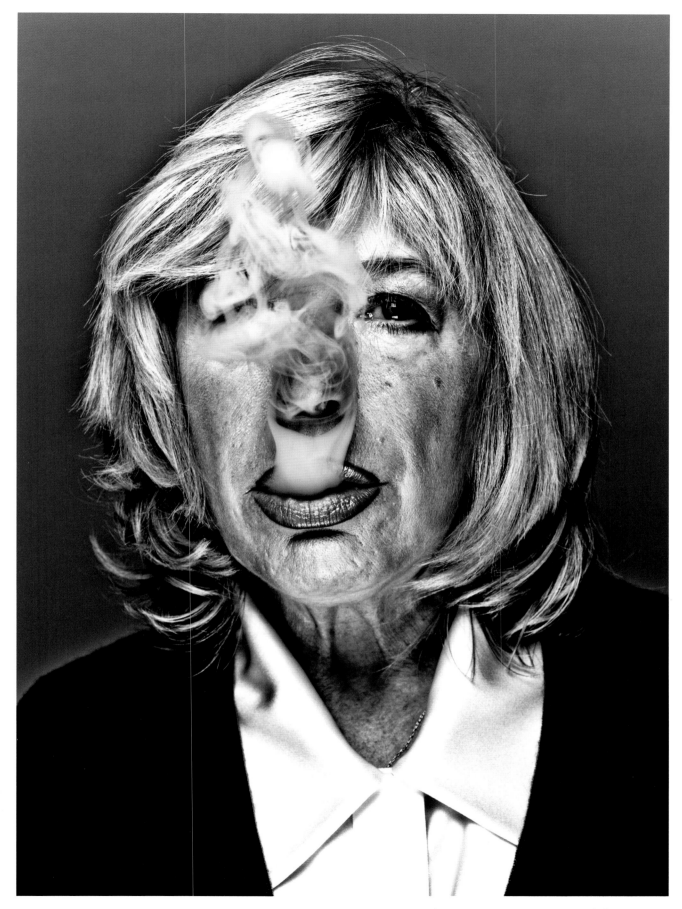

📷: John Wright 🎞: John Wright 📺: Q Magazine

📷: Morgan Silk 👑: Self-promotion

📷: Johann Sebastian Hänel ⌂: Pro7Sat1 In-house, Munich ♛: Pro7Sat1

📷: Mitch Meyer 👑: Self-promotion

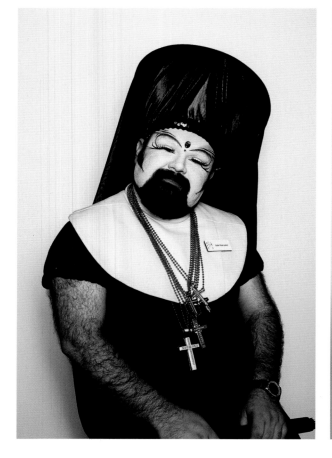

📷: Steve Bonini 🖝: Sally Dadmun 👑: Our House

200bph 10.012

'NATHAN FOLLOWILL

MATTHEW FOLLOWILL

📷: Ray Lego 🔌: Brett Kilroe, Erwin Gorostiza 👑: Sony BMG Music

: Alan Powdrill : Self-promotion

📷: Michael Corridore   🏠: braincells, Claremont, Australia   ✏️: Jeff Chanteloup   👑: Intelligent Life

📷: Sandro ⌂: Starz, Englewood, Colorado 🔌: Kirk Dalton ♛: Self-promotion

📷: Sandro 🔌: Zygmunt Dyrkacz & Lela Headd ♛: Chopin Theatre

📷: Takahito Sato 🎨: Keiichiro Takahashi 🔪: OLFA

📷: Dean Alexander 🔦: Justin Shelby ♛: Federal Hill Fitness

📷: Joan Garrigosa ⌂: Publicis, Barcelona ▭: David Belmonte, David García Navarro ♔: Telefónica

📷: Sylvan Müller & Beat Brechbühl ⌂: FCL In-house, Lucerne ♔: FCL

: David Clerihew ⌂: Intro, London ▭: Julian Gibbs ✎: Intro ♕: Nike Football

📷: Mark Zibert 👑: enRoute Magazine

📷: Vincent Dixon ⌂: BBDO, Atlanta ▱: Justin Lesinsk ♛: AT&T Wireless

📷: Pier Nicola D'Amico ⌂: 72andSunny, Los Angeles ♛: EA Sports

📷: Vincent Dixon ⌒: BBDO, Atlanta ▭►: Justin Lesinsk ♕: AT&T Wireless

📷: Robert Wilson ⌂: Pitch, London 📇: Greg Horton ♕: Skandia Team GBR

📷: Szeling ⌂: Euro RSCG, Singapore 🖊: Hans Ibrahim 👑: 100PLUS

: Sophie Broadbridge ♕: Self-promotion

200bph 10.001

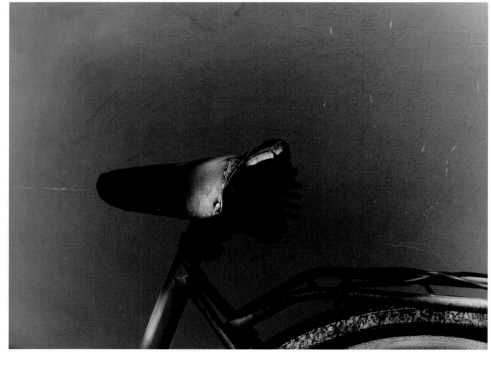

📷: Alex Telfer 👑: Self-promotion

📷: Teo Chai Guan ♔: Self-promotion

📷: Kousaku Hirano 👑: Koyosha + Corabo

⌾: Jenny van Sommers ⑁: Barneys

📷: Fulvio Bonavia ♛: Self-promotion

📷: Kenji Aoki ♔: The New York Times

📷: Joris van Velzen 👑: Nici Theuerkauf

📷: Adrian Mueller ⌂: Lowe, New York ♛: California Milk Processor Board

📷: Bruce Peterson ♔: Self-promotion

📷: Staudinger+Franke ⌂: TMW, London 🎞: Will Kruger 👑: Lipton

📷: Sandro 👑: Self-promotion

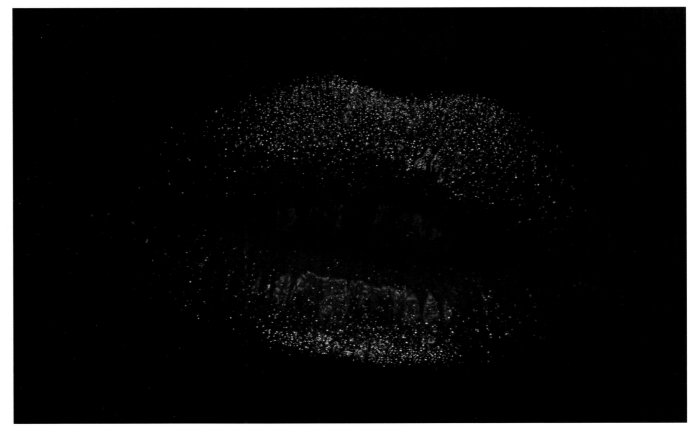

📷: Eric Seow 👑: Self-promotion

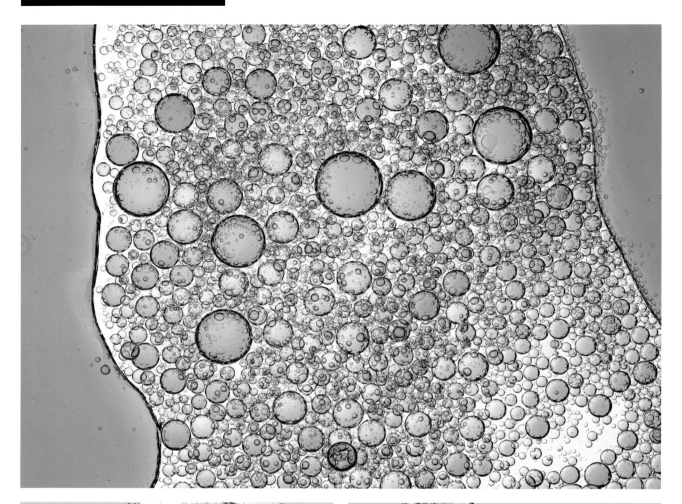

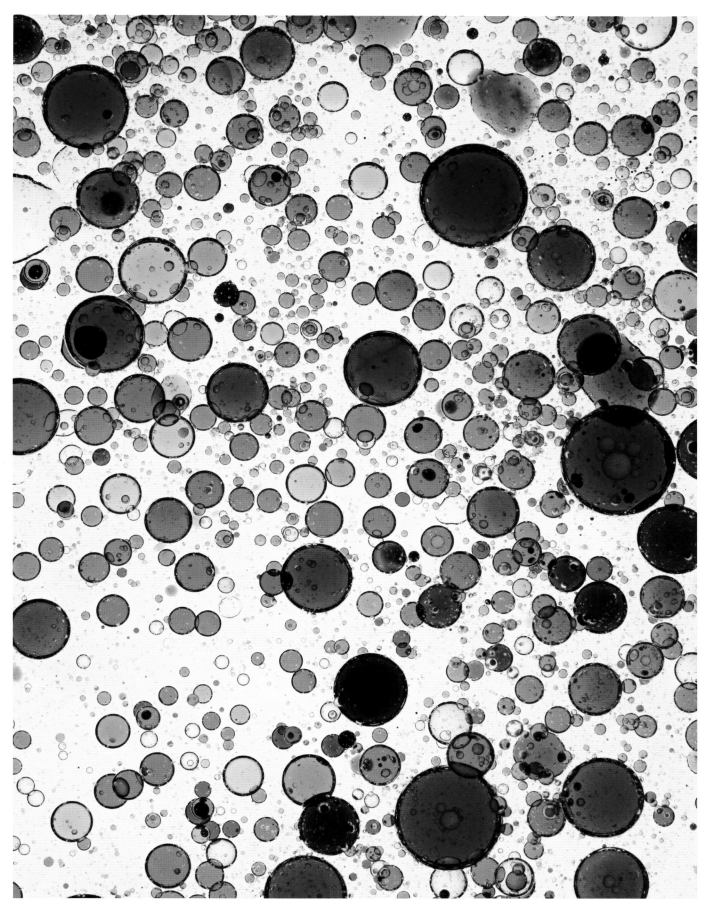

: Jonathan Knowles   : Self-promotion

📷: Kai-Uwe Gundlach 👑: Self-promotion

📷: Robert Tardio 👑: Self-promotion

📷: Jonathan Knowles 👑: Self-promotion

📷: Jacqueline Louter 👑: Self-promotion

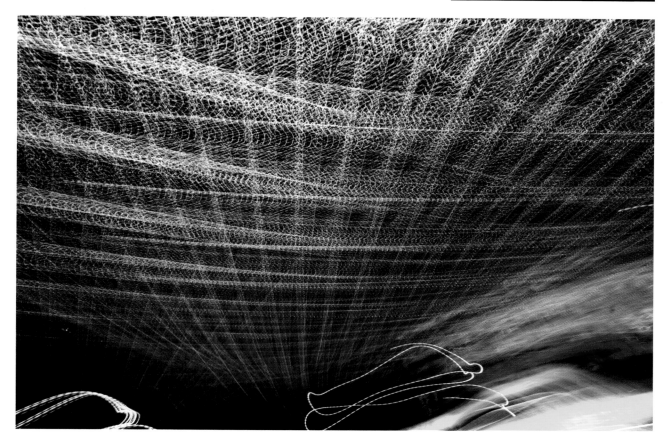

: Uwe Düttmann ♔: Self-promotion

: Eric Seow ⌂: BBDO, Singapore ▭: Gregory Yeo ♔: Eclipse

📷: Christoph Morlinghaus 👑: Self-promotion

: Frank Meyl : IPA Book

📷: Fulvio Bonavia ⌂: Leagas Delaney, Milan ♔: Saab

📷: Ezra Gozo Mansur ▭: Ezra Gozo Mansur ♔: Self-promotion

📷: Michael Corridore ⌂: Publicis Mojo, Sydney ⊏▷: Simon Cox ♔: Lion Nathan

📷: Pete Seaward ♔: Lonely Planet

📷: Andy Glass ⌒: McCann Erickson, Manchester 👑: British Airways

📷: Emir Haveric ⌂: McCann Erickson, San Francisco ✏: Sari Hamman ♕: Microsoft

📷: Daniel Hartz ⌃: Team One, El Segundo, California ▭: James Hendry ♕: Bombardier Flexjet

📷: Andrei Jewell ⌃: Ogilvy & Mather, Singapore 🖾: Kevin Geeves ♕: Castrol

📷: Rory Carter ⌂: Saatchi & Saatchi, Wellington ▭: Samantha Brown ♛: New Zealand Army

📷: Alex Telfer ⌂: Golley Slater, London ▭: David Abbott ♛: British Army

📷: Jaap Vliegenthart ⌂: Rademakkers, Amsterdam 📇: Marc Linderhof 🖌: Jan Stel, Souverein 👑: NVKL

📷: Marc Gouby ⌂: Y&R, Paris 🖦: Sébastien Guinet, Gilles Rivollier 👑: Surfrider Foundation

📷: James Russell 🗨: Ann Rutherford 👑: RRG

📷: Vincent Dixon ⌂: GyroHSR, Chicago ▭: Jeff Clift ♕: Chicago Board Options Exchange

📷: Giuliano Koren 👑: L'espresso

: Wolowski and Partners Studio ⌂: Euro RSCG, Warsaw ▷: Antoni Korzeniowski, Cesar Puebla ♡: Calgon

📷: Tom Nagy ⌂: Ogilvy & Mather, New York/Frankfurt am Main ▭▷: Mark Davis, Christian Leithner ♔: SAP

📷: Tom Nagy ⌂: DDB, Berlin ▭: Johannes Hicks ♕: Volkswagen

📷: Christian Schmidt ⌒: Jung von Matt, Hamburg ▭▷: Oleg Friesen, Deneke von Weltzien ♕: Bitburger

How to get your work published in Lürzer's Archive

You want to submit your ads and posters, TV-Commercials or other advertising materials to Lürzer's Archive? Easy business with Lürzer's Archive online submission system. Simply upload your work at:

www.luerzersarchive.com/submission

Telfer, Alex
Kingsland Church Studios, Priory Green, Byker
NE62DW Newcastle Upon Tyne, United Kingdom
phone: (44) 19 12 65 73 84
fax: (44) 19 12 76 77 78
email: alex@telfer-photography.com
www.alextelfer.com
Representative UK: Peter Bailey Company
phone: (44) 207 935 26 26
www.peterbailey.co.uk
Representative USA: Bill Charles Inc
phone: (1) 212 965 14 65
www.billcharles.com
Representative France: Ask My Agent
phone: (33) 142 72 35 85
www.askmyagent.net
Representative Italy:
Mandala Creative Productions
phone: (39) 02 36 63 57 50
www.mandalacp.it
Representative Hong Kong: The Hive
phone: (852) 34 27 52 17
www.thehive.hk

the unknown artist
C. Martin de los Heros 25
28008 Madrid, Spain
phone: (34) 659 60 23 13
email: mail@t-u-a.org
www.t-u-a.org

The Wade Brothers:
David Lindsey Wade & Lyndon Wade
2010 McGee
64108 Kansas City, USA
phone: (1) 816 421 00 11
fax: (1) 816 421 19 50
www.thewadebrothers.com
Representative: Marge Casey & Associates
www.margecasey.com
Representative: Redorfe
www.redorfe.com

Thymann, Klaus
New York, USA
phone: (1) 212 647 07 77
email: ceo@thymann.com
www.thymann.com
Representative: AFG Management
www.afgmanagement.com

Topelmann, Lars
2626 S.E. Ankeny
97214 Portland, USA
phone: (1) 503 234 19 63
fax: (1) 503 232 68 51
email: lars@larstopelmann.com
www.larstopelmann.com
Representative: Candace Gelman & Associates
www.candacegelman.com

Tran, Robert
Chai Wan, Hong Kong, China
phone: (852) 28 96 26 70
email: robert@roberttran.com
www.roberttran.com

Traylor, Bryan
PO BOX 32022, Camps Bay
Cape Town, South Africa
phone: (27) 822 22 56 23, (27) 214 24 39 86
Representative: Locker 14
email: bryan@locker14.co.za
www.locker14.co.za

van de Beek, Oscar
Tromplaan 42
3742 AD Baarn, The Netherlands
phone: (31) 35 62 80 856
email: oscar@oscarvandebeek.com
www.oscarvandebeek.com
Representative The Netherlands: CreateAgency
www.createagency.nl
Representative Germany: Claudia Bitzer
www.claudiabitzer.de
Representative Spain: pinkorange
www.pinkorange.es
Representative Italy:
Tiziana Gibilisco Photographers
www.photographers.co.it

van Sommers, Jenny
email: mail@jennyvansommers.com
www.jennyvansommers.com
Representative: CLMUK
phone: (44) (0)20 73 13 83 10
www.clmuk.com
Representative: CLMUS
phone: (1) 212 924 65 65
www.clmus.com

van Velzen, Joris
Am Tempelhofer Berg 6
10965 Berlin, Germany
phone: (49) 177 253 48 03
email: info@jorisvanvelzen.com
www.jorisvanvelzen.com

Vigni, Carlo
Via Metastasio, 5
50124 Florence, Italy
email: vigni@catoniassociati.com
email: carlo@carlovigni.com
www.carlovigni.com
Representative: Catoni&Associati
www.catoniassociati.com

Viitala, Antti
Bulevardi 19 E 31
00120 Helsinki, Finland
phone: (358) 500 50 00 87
email: peikko@anttiviitala.com
www.anttiviitala.com
Representative: Oneleague, www.oneleague.co.za

Vives, Jean Marie
5 Villa d'Hauterive
75019 Paris, France
phone: (33) 1 42 25 10 35, fax: (33) 1 42 25 02 15
email: anne.lecerf@watchout.fr
www.watchout.fr
Representative: Watch Out, www.watchout.fr

Vliegenthart, Jaap
Bolstoen 20
1046 Amsterdam, The Netherlands
phone: (31) 20 411 77 35, fax: (31) 20 614 54 96
email: info@jaapvliegenthart.nl
www.jaapvliegenthart.nl
Representative Europe: Unit
www.unit.nl
Representative USA: Monaco Reps
www.monacoreps.com

von Renner, Ivo
Metzendorfer Weg 11
21224 Hamburg, Germany
phone: (41) 08 43 30 00
www.ivofolio.com

von Salomon, Thomas
Schießstättstraße 18-20
80339 Munich, Germany
phone: (49) 172 8 82 49 38, fax: (49) 89 12 00 19 55
email: thomas@vonsalomon.de
www.thomasvonsalomon.com

Vonier, Julien
Binzstrasse 39
8045 Zurich, Switzerland
phone: (41) 44 463 80 10, fax: (41) 44 463 80 34
email: vonier@vonier.ch
www.vonier.ch

Wade, David Lindsey
2010 McGee
64108 Kansas City, USA
phone: (1) 816 421 00 11, fax: (1) 816 421 19 50
email: dlw@davidlindseywade.com
www.davidlindseywade.com
Representative: Marge Casey & Associates
www.margecasey.com
Representative: Redorfe
www.redorfe.com

Wade, Lyndon
2010 McGee
64108 Kansas City, USA
phone: (1) 816 421 00 11, fax: (1) 816 421 19 50
email: lyndon@lyndonwade.com
www.lyndonwade.com
Representative: Marge Casey & Associates
www.margecasey.com
Representative: Redorfe
www.redorfe.com

Watanabe, Shinji
Blackeyes Inc.
3-6-38 505 Nishigotanda, Shinagawaku,
141-0031 Tokyo, Japan
phone: (81) 80 6506 9604
mail: watanabe@blackeyes.co.jp
www.blackeyes.co.jp

Westerby, Mark
United Kingdom
phone: (44) 796 646 73 15
email: info@markwesterby.com
www.markwesterby.com
Representative: Expose
phone: (44) 20 89 87 60 53
www.expose-productions.co.uk

Wilson, Robert
London, United Kingdom
phone: (44) 785 023 25 80
email: robert@robertjwilson.com
www.robertjwilson.com
Representative UK: Catherine Collins
phone: (44) 20 77 39 86 78
www.catherinecollins.co.uk
Representative Germany: G.S. Abroad
phone: (44) 20 89 92 05 70
www.gsabroad.com
Representative USA: Tim Mitchell
phone: (1) 781 631 52 35
www.t-mitchell.com

Wohlwender, Steven
1330 Rainbow Drive
94402 San Mateo, USA
phone: (1) 650 350 17 73
email: s@stevenwohlwender.com
www.stevenwohlwender.com
Representative: Held & Associates
www.cynthiaheld.com

Wolowski and Partners Studio
Raclawicka 99
02-634 Warsaw, Poland
email: studio@wolowski.com.pl,
www.wolowski.com.pl
Representative: Jacek Wolowski
www.wolowski.com.pl

Wong, Jeremy
5 Upper Aljunied Link, #07-03,
Quartz Industrial Building
367903 Singapore, Singapore
phone: (65) 62 81 38 81
fax: (65) 62 81 38 82
Representative: Nemesis Pictures
email: jeremy@nemesispictures.com.sg
www.nemesispictures.com.sg

Wood, Josh
608 East Wilmington Avenue
84106 Sugarhouse, USA
phone: (1) 801 452 52 24
email: info@joshwoodphotography.com
www.joshwoodphotography.com

Woodward, Scott A.
83 Hillview Avenue, #03-05 Meralodge
669583 Singapore, Singapore
phone: (65) 9336 35 26
email: scott@scottawoodward.com
www.scottawoodward.com

Wright, John
London, United Kingdom
phone: (44) 844 736 26 31
fax: (44) 844 736 27 16
email: production@johnwrightphoto.com
www.johnwrightphoto.com

Yang, Peter
144 N 7th Street #415
11211 New York, USA
phone: (1) 646 290 67 96
fax: (1) 646 607 37 00
email: studio@peteryang.com,
www.peteryang.com
Representative: Greenhouse Reps
www.greenhousereps.com

Zakharova, Alexandra & Plotnikov, Ilya
3 Sokolinoi Gory Str.
Moscow, Russia
phone: (7) 905 756 06 96
Representative: Dobermanstudio
email: box@dobermanstudio.ru
www.dobermanstudio.ru

Zibert, Mark
Canada
phone: (1) 416 469 49 00
email: mark@markzibert.com
www.markzibert.com
Representative USA: Vaughn Hannigan
www.vh-artists.com
Representative Europe: Zeynep
www.zeyneprepresents.com
Representative Canada: JK Reps Inc.,
www.jkreps.com

Zona13
Via Mecenate 76/25
20138 Milan, Italy
phone: (39) 02 87 39 20 97
fax: (39) 02 87 39 20 04
email: info@zona13.com
www.zona13photo.com
Representative: Mandala cp, www.mandalacp.it